THE PEDAGOGICS OF UNLEARNING

Before you start to read this book, take this moment to think about making a donation to punctum books, an independent non-profit press,

@ https://punctumbooks.com/support/

If you're reading the e-book, you can click on the image below to go directly to our donations site. Any amount, no matter the size, is appreciated and will help us to keep our ship of fools afloat. Contributions from dedicated readers will also help us to keep our commons open and to cultivate new work that can't find a welcoming port elsewhere. Our adventure is not possible without your support.
Vive la open-access.

Fig. 1. Hieronymus Bosch, *Ship of Fools* (1490–1500)

THE PEDAGOGICS OF UNLEARNING Copyright © 2016 Editors and authors. This work carries a Creative Commons BY-NC-SA 4.0 International license, which means that you are free to copy and redistribute the material in any medium or format, and you may also remix, transform, and build upon the material, as long as you clearly attribute the work to the authors and editors (but not in a way that suggests the authors or punctum books endorses you and your work), you do not use this work for commercial gain in any form whatsoever, and that for any remixing and transformation, you distribute your rebuild under the same license. http://creativecommons.org/licenses/by-nc-sa/4.0/

First published in 2016 by punctum books, Earth, Milky Way.
www. punctumbooks.com

ISBN-13: 978-0692722343
ISBN-10: 0692722343
Library of Congress Cataloging Data is available from the Library of Congress

Cover image: Andrew Loxley
Cover and title page design: Chris Piuma
Type design: Vincent W.J. van Gerven Oei

the pedagogics of **unlearning**

Aidan Seery +
Éamonn Dunne
editors

punctum books
earth, milky way

Contents

Learning to Unlearn · 13
Éamonn Dunne

Un-What? · 25
Jacques Rancière

Phantasies of the Writing Block: A Psychoanalytic
Contribution to Pernicious Unlearning · 47
Deborah Britzman

Learning How to Be a Capitalist: From Neoliberal Pedagogy to the Mystery of Learning · 73
Samuel A. Chambers

Teaching the Event: Deconstruction, Hauntology,
and the Scene of Pedagogy · 111
John D. Caputo

The Intimate Schoolmaster and the Ignorant *Sifu*:
Poststructuralism, Bruce Lee, and the
Ignorance of Everyday Radical Pedagogy · 131
Paul Bowman

Unlearning: A Duologue · 157
L.O. Aranye Fradenburg & Eileen A. Joy

After-word(s) · 189
Aidan Seery

Acknowledgments

This book arises from *The Pedagogics of Unlearning* conference held at Trinity College Dublin in September 2014. Our speakers included Lauren Berlant, Paul Bowman, Deborah Britzman, Sam Chambers, Aranye Fradenburg, Jack Halberstam, Eileen Joy, Jacques Rancière, and Nick Royle. For their overwhelming generosity, incisive responses and good humor, and on behalf of the organizers, we would like to thank them all. They made those few days in Dublin an extraordinary, exquisite, and unforgettable experience.

We would like to sincerely thank punctum books and Eileen Joy for co-sponsoring the event and Vincent W.J. van Gerven Oei and Chris Piuma for a brilliant job typesetting and designing the book; also, Andrew Loxley for the original image. We were also immensely grateful to Victor Taylor, Carl Raschke, the Global Art & Ideas Nexus (GAIN) and the *Journal for Cultural and Religious Theory* for their generous sponsorship. Thanks also to the artist Sam Keogh for the original image advertising the conference. A big thanks is also due to Deborah Withers and Alex Wardrop for including the "Irrationale" for *The Pedagogics of Unlearning* event in the recently published *Para-Academic Handbook* from HammerOn Press.

Deepest gratitude is also due to Katie Guinnane for helping out with all things administrative and to Jon Mitchell, Tina Kinsella, Saundre McConney, Ger Dunne, and Graham Price, whose company and commitment have been superb. To Lian McGuire and Valerie Kelly in the School of Education at TCD, thank you kindly for supporting us. To CAVE (Cultures, Academic Values and Education Research Centre), profound and heartfelt gratitude for supporting this endeavor. Others (teachers and friends) who have, knowingly or unknowingly, influenced this endeavor include: Carol Buckley, Anne Clarke, Adrienne Colgan, Donal Evoy, Ruairi Farrell, Martin Healy, Ger Hughes, Terence A. Halpin, Elaine Jenkinson, Conor Kennedy, Stephanie Kinsella, Gus Lynch, Bill Maher, Gareth McRory, Rosaleen Montes-Silva, Kathy Reilly, and Sean OSuilleabhain.

*For Michael O'Rourke, mentor, colleague, and close close friend
— nothing happens without you.*

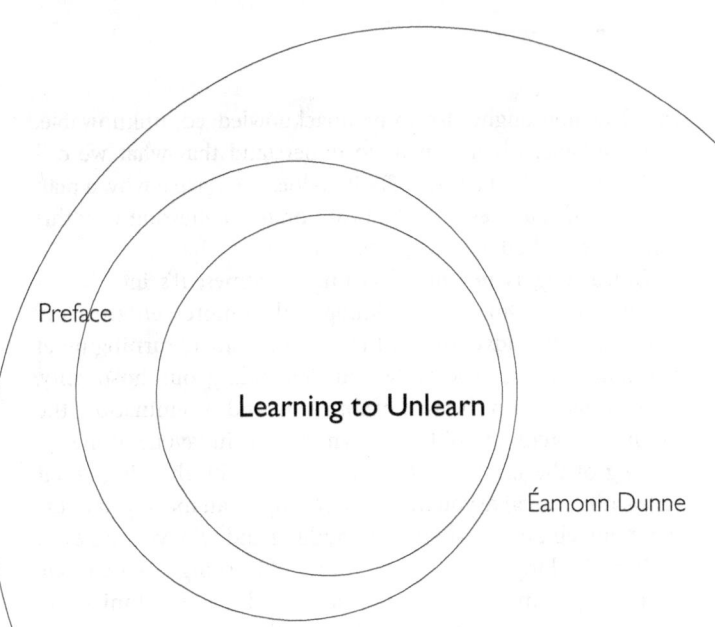

Preface

Learning to Unlearn

Éamonn Dunne

Since this is a book concerning a certain "pedagogics of unlearning," there is no real reason why I should approach my task of introducing a collection of essays on that topic in anything like a conventional manner. If I was to be really responsible to the call of this question — the question of what unlearning essentially means — I would also have to be (however impossibly) wholly irresponsible. I would have to invent it anew. I would have to invent a concept of unlearning that holds true for each of the following essays. This is impossible, since each essay approaches this question singularly, uniquely, and with its own eye towards the range and scope of education.

This is why the call to unlearning insinuates a kind of originality and invention, of finding something new and discovering something old within the new for the first time. Furthermore, it resounds with notions of betrayal, of perversity and of a reluctance to settle for the soporific balm of the familiar at all costs. Unlearning calls on us to shake things up, to shake it off, to philosophize with a hammer, to take a leap of faith into the abyss of nonknowledge; it calls on us to let go, to fail, to fail again, for better or for worse. It calls on us to take the risk that encounters with learning ought also to be unacknowledged, unknowable, unassimilable. It calls on us to understand that what we call learning (*Was Heißt Lernen?*) often does not have a why, a plan or an agenda, and essentially it calls on us to question why this is the case, or better, why this *takes* place.

Unlearning is not into learning *out*comes; it's into learning *in*comes. It's into the incoming of the unforeseen, the truly monstrous, the advent of all those wholly others turning up at our doorsteps unexpectedly and demanding our hospitality. Unlearning is *in*to the risk of intrusion and insemination, the insolent overcoming of the known knowns in favour of the *in*-coming of the unknown knowns. This is why thinking about unlearning can give you indigestion; why it can make you question yourself and what you are thinking and why you are even "doing" thinking. Whatever your idea of learning is — be it one of emancipation or one of stultification, of latitude or limitation, of masters or of bondsmen — the question of unlearning worries your clean categorizations, takes you out of your comfort zone, beyond your limits, turning them outside *in* rather that inside out.

Unlearning's semantic force does not pretend to be the antithesis of learning. Whatever that could be? Neither does its peculiar force reside in a simple linguistic slippage, as if semantic questions where somehow divorced from the referential real world of the here and now. We can't simply claim, that is, that "unlearning" is just another word for something we've been saying all along elsewhere and are now only coming around to explaining. In fact what "unlearning" gives us is another starting point, a fulcrum, a place to investigate what exactly we think we mean by "learning," where we are going with this idea, where we have been going with it all along, and where we plan to go with it in the future.

My gambit (a gambit which each of the following pieces picks up) is that once "unlearning" becomes a question for "learning" we are in a very difficult place indeed. We are in a place we don't necessarily want to be. This is precisely why we need to think about what we mean by this wonderfully elusive, allusive, even illusive word. It ought to be enough then to mention that when we speak of unlearning we are not in the realm of the known. We are certainly not in the realm of simplistic binaries or structured hierarchies in the artifice of education. To think of unlearning is to begin to think about how we have become used to learning, so used to it in fact that we have failed to even question it.

"There is a need for interrupting the politics of learning," claims Gert Biesta in a beautiful new book about learning and education, a need to "denaturalize the idea of learning" (Biesta 2013, 76). We need interruption because we have become immune to criticizing something that has for so long been a simple, unquestionable given. Learning has become immured in learning. We learn *all* the time. We learn without knowing that we are learning. We even learn as we breathe, simply and progressively, passively and penitently. Learning in this thinking has become yet another word for osmosis. It's just something we do and are ultimately done in by.

According to this narrative learning is risk free, at once a process term and an individualistic term, progressive and personal, unending, private. Since the 1990s the language of learning has become ubiquitous in educational policy, research and practice. We are now in the "age of learning" where learning is the key to success, fulfilment and personal growth. We are considered autonomous subjects, "lifelong learners," consumers and producers of our own education (Biesta 2013). The "learnification" of education is Biesta's coinage for the omniscience of the learning agenda and our continuing failure to politicize and challenge its hegemony. It is the learning discourse fuelled by the notion that what we need is more and more learning, that society and the individual will progress through learning goals and outcomes to a cleaner, better, faster future. Just keep learning, keep pumping money into your learning, keep young minds passing through institutions at astronomical rates, and things will just happen for the better; the just will just come to fulfil the promise of the democracy to come. Of course the learning agenda is heavily politicized; yet we are failing all the time to notice it in both practice and theory.

When we refer to "learning" we are not using a passive descriptor, however we may think about it. We are engaged in normative judgements. Learning discourses, that is to say, are not simply *descriptive* discourses; they are strongly *evaluative* conceptualizations. Think about the languages we are using for all of this: we talk about "teaching and learning"; we teach in "learning-friendly environments"; our students are "learners" and we are "facilitators of learning"; our teaching is geared towards "learning outcomes"; we stress AFL ("assessment for learning") strategies in our classrooms; and ultimately we progress through the status of "adult learners" until death do us part from all our learning(s). But do we stop to consider if learning is what *education* ought to be about? "In my more radical moments," says Biesta, "I sometimes even think that learning is the last thing educators should be concerned about" (2013, 59). This is grist for the mill of unlearners; learning ought to be questioned and its processes put under erasure. We need to conceive of learning without the outcome. Even more radically, we need to start asking ourselves about its subliminal purposes, about why "learning" has become the *conditio sine qua non* of education, where the promise of the word "education" has become erased and forgotten like a face drawn in the sand at the edge of a sea (Foucault 1994, 387). We need to start asking why and when learning became a synonym for "education" and why and where that education is now directed.

Let's think about learning a little more conventionally for a moment. The primary sense of the verb "to learn" stems from an Old English word *leornian* and the Old High German word *lernen*. It relates to the acquisition of knowledge or the attainment of a skill through study, experience, or teaching. No surprises there. But there ought to be. If we are honest, our experiences of education tell us time and time again that learning surprises us; that it takes us over, undoes our perspectives and radically changes our world views. My hypothesis here is that you ought to be surprised by this *continually,* every moment of every day, every time you teach or think about teaching or learning. That's our Mount Moriah, our impossible moment of deciding what to do in a moment of crisis. If thinking about learning as an activity is undertaken carefully, conscientiously, rigorously, then thinking about thinking should be premised on the surprise and event of that activity; it ought to be premised on questions like: what does it mean to understand understanding? How does thinking in taking place take the place(s) of preconditioned, installed ideologemes of thinking? How can we think, to play off Emmanuel Levinas, other*wise* than being and beyond knowledge? How does thinking unlearn itself? How do we learn to unlearn?

If we are to think seriously about learning then we ought to think about the way that learning happens as a disruptive, unsettling, or better, an interruptive force. We need to plug hope into a future that will change our very idea of learning: "Learning is [in fact] conditioned by hope, something unforeseen that one, nevertheless, expects" (Joldersma 2014, 39). In a sense learning is impossible, since for learning to happen, we need to expect the unexpected; we need to learn to unlearn. That is to say, "learning starts with unlearning [*Entlernen*]" (Hamacher 2004, 171).

There's a beautifully subtle reading from Hegel back to Plato and Aristotle, from Jean-Luc Nancy in *Being Singular Plural*, which provocatively maintains that philosophy is precisely this: "surprised thought" [*la pensée surprise*]. "We need to think," Nancy claims, "about how thought can and must be surprised — and how it may be exactly this that makes it think. Or then again we need to think about how there would be no thought without the event of thinking" (Nancy 2000, 165). This means that the event of thinking is actually an impediment to teaching what thinking is. Or, to be more precise, if thinking is surprised thought, then learning is suspended over an abyss of unlearning and that unlearning can happen only as the event of an-other understanding. To love thinking, to speak *philo*sophically, means to love the surprise of thought. It means being in love with the unsettling *in*sistence of unlearning.[1] To really love

---

1 See John D. Caputo's essay below and also his *The Insistence of God: A Theology of Perhaps* (Bloomington: Indiana University Press, 2013).

learning means opening yourself up to the event and to the hope that something might come to help you stage the becoming of another you and another us.

A subsidiary sense of the verb "to learn" refers specifically to an act of memory. This latter sense is present when we say things in our classrooms like "do you recall how Gatsby acquired his fortune?" or "does everyone remember why Jude wanted to learn Latin?" or in direct past-tense constructions like "I got it" or "I learnt it by heart." Learning by heart is a wonderful phrase for acts of memory. The phrase compresses the notion of acquisition into a temporal vacuum. But it also spirals into questions of sense and sensibility. Does it mean that I understand or that I feel something? Does it mean both simultaneously? Or does it mean one or the other intermittently? If I learn a poem by heart, for instance, does it mean I acquire its meaning, that I can summarize it, or does it mean that I don't know what it essentially means for others, *only* for me? After all, it's my heart, right? Though we speak of the "heart of the matter" it's not necessarily the same thing (is it?) as saying, "I've learnt something by heart;" that I *feel* (not necessarily think about) something in my deep heart's core?

One of the best places to begin investigating the phrase "learning by heart" is Jacques Derrida's strangely elliptical little piece called "Che cos'è la poesia?" Nicholas Royle calls this tiny essay "one of Derrida's most lapidary performatives or *perverformatives*"; it's a little gem (Royle 2003, 98). Like in "Learning to live finally," Derrida's last interview, "Che cos'è la poesia?" focuses on what that phrase "to learn by heart" might mean. The piece is the more unusual, though no less impassioned, for Derrida's refusal to settle into any real logical argument. It abounds in all sorts of peculiar, playful repetitions, allusions, counterpaths, blind alleys, and obscure crevices. What "Che cos'è la poesia?" essentially does is teach us by withholding from us what we want to know. It is an exercise in the undoing of the known, of the teaching of poetry that is other*wise*.

Throughout "Che cos'è la poesia?" Derrida pushes the phrase "to learn by heart" into obscure regions. In French to "learn by heart" is *apprendre par cœur*. The word *apprendre*, as Nick Royle has pointed out, carries the sense "to teach," and "to hear," as well as "to learn" (Royle 2003, 136). Like the word "apprehend" in English it has the sense that something is grasped, held, arrested, understood or perceived in a fixed state. This is dangerous. It's dangerous because learning by heart is also a correlative of "learning by rote," the unthinking, vacuous rendering of information for information's sake, a desire to fashion urns out of texts. But, as Derrida has it, the poem doesn't hold still in words; it's like a body in movement, a lateral dance across the page. This allusiveness instills jealousy, a desire to want to have it and have done with it, to "know how to forget knowledge [...] to set fire to the library." Hence Derrida's neat paradox, "You must celebrate; you have to commemorate amnesia, savagery, even the stupidity of the by-heart" (Derrida 1995, 297).

In a peculiar turnabout Derrida claims that it is the poem that teaches the heart, that invents the heart. It is the poem that teaches us how to read, to learn, to feel and to forget. The experience of learning *by* heart, of learning *the* heart, derails knowledge, upsets subjectivity, worries the selfhood of self, the *Dasein* of *Sein*. The experience of the event of the poem (the poem as event) exposes us to chance, to risk and to uncertainty, and to wonder, ignorance and stupidity. "Poems, therefore, befall us like benedictions; benedictions come from the other, the coming of the other" (Derrida 1995, 297). You can't teach that kind of learning. The heart has to learn that for itself. This is why, as an act of faith, a benediction if you like, I believe you can't teach anyone how to read, not at least methodologically, since reading, like poetry, undoes its own definition. Reading, by which I mean good reading, has to be a matter of the heart as well as the head. It's a matter of learning how to read between the lines.

The word "unlearning" is a disjunctive register that catches something of the pace of this thinking, as opposed to perhaps, "understanding," which is an apprehensive word. Let me repeat this. The word does not signify as a direct antonym of "learning." This is its sheer peculiarity and potentiality — the most important issue for us to think through. You don't have learning on the one hand and unlearning on the other. Unlearning doesn't sediment ignorance and stupidity as the obverse of teaching and learning. Learning does not contradict unlearning and vice versa; there is no either/or whereby we might contrast the two. At its weakest, unlearning is simply synonymous with learning. Unlearning's perversity and irrationality, the fact that it doesn't mean any-thing, any one-thing, causes minor insurrections for people like Avital Ronell, Jack Caputo, Barbara Johnson, J. Hillis Miller, and Werner Hamacher — all of whose works intermittently obsess over this idea. Learning begins when knowledge gets suspended. Good teachers are teachers who suspend knowledge, who open up the abyss. They're the ones that know that counselling Enlightenment values of self-reliance and autonomy initiate an inescapable double bind. "Listen to me but don't listen to me." "Listen to me: Think for yourself!" *Sapere aude.* Some instruction! Good teachers know that teaching and learning is not an endpoint, not a goal towards autonomy. There's always more to be gained from dialogism and from the asymmetry of the face-to-face encounter. Effective teachers are the ones, as Ronell says, who can say, "I am stupid before the other," who are comfortable with a certain "foolosophy" and who know (without fully knowing why) stupidity and ignorance are not antithetical to concepts of intelligence and knowledge (Ronell 2004, 55).[2] The ones who dismantle the *sujet supposé savoir* — the one who is supposed to know.

The "un" in unlearning is like the "un" in Freud's *unheimlich*, at once both strange and familiar. Like the uncanny, unlearning resonates with questions of limits and borders — semantic, epistemological, philosophical, ontological, esoteric and aesthetic. Like Freud's term, it's about what is familiar to us and unfamiliar simultaneously. You might think that you know what it is to learn, but if you ask yourself what is the opposite of learning you have to face up to the quasi-antonymic register, "unlearning." Though we might think of the prefix in the negative sense, in re-

---

2 For more on the concept of "foolosophy" see my "Love Foolosophy: Pedagogy, Parable, Perversion," *Educational Philosophy and Theory* 45, no. 6 (2013).

ality the "un" in unlearning signals a more difficult knowledge. You might call it a kind of untology. Examples also exist, according to the OED, where "un" is used conversely as a positive.

Orthographical concerns aside, I'm not trying out a kind of archaeology as a theory of what unlearning is, a theory that might lead us to a methodology of unlearning. With this in mind, and within such space constraints, I can only give three propositions along with three examples, which I think explain the case of unlearning. The essays which follow in this book will present their own retellings of what unlearning is and is not, but for now permit me to conclude with three older ones. Here they are:

Proposition 1: Teaching someone how to read literature is impossible

Example: Barbara Johnson

> Teaching reading is teaching how to read. How to notice things in a text that a speed-reading culture is trained to disregard, overcome edit out, or explain away; how to read what the language is doing, not guess what the author was thinking; how to take in evidence from the page, not seek a reality to substitute for it. This is the only teaching that can properly be called literary; anything else is history of ideas, biography, psychology, ethics or bad philosophy. Anything else does not measure up to the rigorous perversity of literary language (Johnson 1988, 68).

Proposition 2: Teaching is just without reason

Example: Bill Readings

> No authority can terminate the pedagogic relation, no knowledge can save us the task of thinking [...] We must seek to do justice to teaching rather than to know what it is. A belief that we know what teaching is or should be is actually a major im-

pediment to just teaching. Teaching should cease to be about merely the transmission of information and the emancipation of the autonomous subject, and instead should become a site of obligation that exceeds an individual's consciousness of justice. My turn to the pedagogical scene of address, with all its ethical weight, is thus a way of developing an accountability at odds with accounting (Readings 1996, 154).

Proposition 3: Ignorance does not mean failure

Example: Interview with Orson Welles, BBC 1960

> Interviewer: Where did you get the confidence to make *Citizen Kane*?
>
> Welles: Ignorance, ignorance, sheer ignorance. You know there's no confidence to equal it. It's only when you know something about a profession, I think, that you're timid, or careful.
>
> Interviewer: How does this ignorance show itself?
>
> Welles: I thought you could do anything with a camera that the eye could do, that the imagination could do. And if you come up from the bottom in the film business you're taught all the things that the cameraman shouldn't attempt for fear you might be criticized for having failed. And in this case I had a cameraman who didn't care if he was criticized if he failed and I didn't know there were things you couldn't do, so anything I could think up in my dreams I attempted to photograph, not knowing that they were impossible or theoretically impossible. And again I had a real advantage not only in the real genius of my cameraman but in the fact that he, like all great men I think who are masters of their craft told me right from the start, there was nothing about camera work that I couldn't learn in half a day, that any intelligent person couldn't learn in half a day. And he was right. The great

mystery that requires twenty years doesn't exist in any field, certainly not the camera (Welles 1960).

Learning from these extracts means learning about the event. And I emphasise the word "about" here. It means learning *about* the event's openness to futurity, to the to-come, to a radical hermeneutics resistant to the dogmatic slumber of acquired (required) understanding; the tyranny of institutionalization and the concept of winning at all costs, of excellence over Thought (Readings 1996, 150–165). The eventness of the event, our failure to pin it down in the here and now, like a Zeno paradox, ensures that we are as ever alive to the trace of learning in the *living time* of learning, which is also a mode of unlearning. In this unlearning signifies the renewal of understanding in terms of what Schlegel called *Unverständlichkeit,* an un-understandability at the beating heart of each and every enunciation, its performativity — or more justly its perverformativity (Schlegel 1964). If quotidian scenes of teaching and learning instruct us experientially, they do so by constantly renewing and emphasizing singularity and unexpectedness. This is what, I wager, constitutes the most intense form of unlearning.

If there is a law applicable to the concept (non-concept) of unlearning then it is simply this: That in teaching you can never be sure what you are teaching or precisely what effect you are having on your students, or when that effect will manifest itself, when it will return, how it will return, from where it will return. This does not absolve us from our responsibilities to teach. In fact, it intensifies them, hyperbolizes them. Knowing not what you do is no excuse for not knowing that what you do often has far-reaching consequences. The task is to know that this is the case and to try, as far as possible, to keep opening learning to debate, to make thinking about teaching an *event* and a new locus of learning. This book is a beginning and a plea to teachers everywhere to learn to unlearn, however impossibly.

REFERENCES

Biesta, G. (2013). *The Beautiful Risk of Education*. London: Paradigm.

Derrida, J. (1995) *Points…: Interviews, 1974–1994*, trans. Peggy Kamuf et al. Stanford: Stanford University Press.

Dunne, É. (2013). "Love Foolosophy: Pedagogy, Parable, Perversion." *Educational Philosophy and Theory* 45.6.

Foucault, M. (1994). *The Order of Things: An Archaeology of the Human Sciences*, trans. Alan Sheridan-Smith. New York: Vintage Books.

Hamacher, W. (2004). "To Leave the Word to Someone Else." In *Thinking Difference: Critics in Conversation*, ed. Julian Wolfreys. Edinburgh: Edinburgh University Press.

Johnson, B. (1988). *A World of Difference*. Baltimore: Johns Hopkins University Press.

Joldersma, C.W. (2014). *A Levinasian Ethics for Education's Commonplaces: Between Calling and Inspiration*. New York: Palgrave.

Nancy, J.L. (2000). *Being Singular Plural*, trans. Robert D. Richardson et al. Stanford: Stanford University Press.

Readings, B. (1996). *The University in Ruins*. Cambridge: Harvard University Press.

Ronell, A. (2004). "Confessions of an Anacoluthon: On Writing, Technology, Pedagogy, and Politics." In *Thinking Difference: Critics in Conversation*, ed. Julian Wolfreys. Edinburgh: Edinburgh University Press.

Royle, N. (2003). *Jacques Derrida*. London: Routledge.

Schlegel, F. (1964). "Über die Unverständlichkeit." In *Kritische Schriften*, ed. Wolfdietrich Rasch, 530–42. Munich: Karl Hanser Verlag.

Welles, O. (1960). "Huw Wheldon Interviews Orson Welles on *Citizen Kane*." BBC Monitor Show. See https://www.youtube.com/watch?v=bbSqsStlLpA.

Un-What?

Jacques Rancière

Pedagogics of Unlearning: the title of this conference obviously echoes a notion and a figure that I had set up in my own way when I published a book entitled *The Ignorant Schoolmaster* with the subtitle *Five Lessons in Intellectual Emancipation* (Rancière 1991). Both titles entail the idea of a specific form of learning, which is a negative one: learning how to unlearn, teaching as an ignorant, learning the emancipatory virtue of ignorance. This idea raises two interrelated problems: firstly, how are we to understand the type of negativity at work in this "unlearning" or this "ignorance"? Secondly, what is the exact target of this negative action? What is the positivity that is under attack? In other terms, what is at stake in matters of learning?

Let us first tackle the issue of negativity. I wish to emphasize what the negativity entailed in the "ignorance" of the ignorant schoolmaster is not. It is not a method of the *tabula rasa*, asking us to start again from scratch. It is not a question of finding the right way of acquiring the knowledge, in the Cartesian manner, by getting rid of all the opinions, judgments and prejudices that we had previously accepted. The reason for this is simple: even though the method of the *tabula rasa* challenges the established edifice of knowledge and the institutional forms of learning, it shares with them one fundamental principle: the principle that there is *one* point from which we must start and one definite order that we must follow to acquire knowledge in the right way. I recall it in passing: it is also the belief that is shared by most of the alternative — and even libertarian — theories and practices of pedagogy. And it is also the belief that is shared by most of the revolutionary theories when they denounce the role of the educational institutions in the system of domination.

No *tabula rasa* therefore. From the point of view of intellectual emancipation, there is only one opinion of which we must get rid — an opinion that unfortunately most of the radical methods forget to get rid of: the opinion of inequality. This statement forces us to engage in a close examination of the two terms (opinion and inequality) and of their connection. The opinion of inequality is not the opinion that human beings are unequal for this or that reason. An opinion is not what it is readily told to be: a vague judgment present in our minds — and notably in uneducated minds — about things of which we have no clear knowledge. Instead it is the very framework within which we get educated and acquire knowledge. Such is the great discovery that we owe to Jacotot: the opinion of inequality is not a matter of judgments. It is a matter of structures. It is the framework within which we learn and know, within which the work of our mind is linked with that of all the other minds, within which, in short, the exercise of our intellectual capacity comes into agreement with the inequality of the social order.

This coincidence between the exercise of our intellectual capacity and the unequal social order has been summed up by Jacotot in one single notion: *explanation*. This simple word implies a whole framing of the intellectual world according to two principles that I will spell out briefly, by both following Jacotot and translating his argumentation in my own terms: a principle of *extensiveness* and a principle of *progressiveness*. I wish to examine their general formula before investigating the transformations that each of them has undergone since his time and the new forms of their interconnection. In both cases I think that this general formula is best understood *a contrario*. That's why I'll try to define the two principles of the explanatory system by contrast with the two principles that Jacotot pit against them: *Everything is in everything* and *Learn something and relate to it all the rest by this principle: all men have equal intelligence* (Rancière 1991, 18, 41–43). Learn *something*: this very simple order is enough to shatter the logic of explanation. For the latter precisely says: you cannot learn *something*. As long as you are before "something," you are before an opaque particularity which has its reason outside itself. You are before an opaque fragment of an unknown totality. You cannot learn anything unless you understand its connection to the whole of which it is a fragment. The problem is that this "whole" has no delimitation. There is always a link that is lacking to catch up with it. Only those who have the knowledge of the whole can show you the relation of anything to "all the rest." This whole is of course unpresentable. This means that it must be presupposed as inherent to the power of making the links, to the capacity of those who know how to know. Now this capacity in turn is demonstrated in a very specific way: it is demonstrated out of the incapacity of those who don't know how to know: those who are before the thing and don't see the link. Understanding the relation thus amounts to understanding inequality. You cannot learn anything without learning the inequality of intelligence: the inequality between the intelligence of those who see the connections of the whole and the intelligence of those who are enclosed in the relation of a private — idiotic — mind to particular things.

This difference is also a difference between two forms of temporality. That difference has been spelled out long ago in Aristotle's *Poetics*: on the one side, there is the chronicle which tells how events happen, in their particularity, one after another; on the other side, there is the poetic plot, which tells how those events have been possible, according to the rules of necessity or verisimilitude. This is the difference of temporalities which is both set at work and denied by the second principle of the explanatory logic: the logic of progressiveness. Once again we can best understand it *a contrario* out of the Jacototian "learn something."

The point is that the explanatory logic on its part always says: learn *such thing* and then *such other thing*. The distance between "something" and the whole can only be covered by following a definite order. This definite order is a definite correspondence between the unfolding of time and the unfolding of knowledge. Such a correspondence also presupposes the existence of a privileged knowledge of the whole: not only the knowledge of the connections that constitute it but the knowledge of the progression according to which the ignoramus is able to make this or that step in his travel — in short the knowledge of ignorance or the knowledge of the inequality of intelligence.

Such is the knowledge that is "transmitted" to the student with any new piece of knowledge: the knowledge of his/her incapacity to know how to move from one step to the next one. Progressiveness is the way in which the gap between the two temporalities is managed: on the one hand, the gap is denied: the distance between ignorance and knowledge is told to be a mere matter of time: the time of education is the time within which the distance will be suppressed. On the other hand, each step in that progression reopens the gap between those who live in the time of the things happening one after another and those who have the intelligence of the whole. This is how the two principles are in accordance. In a way the principle of progressiveness is only a consequence of the inegalitarian logic contained in the principle of extensiveness. But, at the same time, it is the principle that makes it a social institution: the institution whose timetable is specifically devoted to the relation between ignorance and knowledge. The schooling system gives an institutional framework to the presupposition of a coincidence between three times: the time of the acquisition of knowledge, the time of development of the individuals and the time of development of the society — which means that it gives an institutional framework to the reproduction of the opinion of inequality under the guise of the progress of the individuals toward knowledge and of the progress of society toward equality.

In short, "explanation" means much more than a specific academic exercise. It is the configuration of a whole world of experience. It gives it its topography (principle of extensiveness) and its timetable (principle of progressiveness). This is why what has to be unlearned is much more than a matter of pedagogical methods. Intellectual emancipation is not an alternative pedagogy for two reasons. First, the "learn something and relate to it all the rest" and the "everything is in everything" do not define the right method for teaching and learning. Instead they dismiss the very idea of the right method: all *right* methods are in keeping with the principles of explanation and stultification: they all boast on knowing how to know. Therefore they all propose to start from the right point of departure and to follow the right order. They all share the presupposition of this whole which is at the same time given and subtracted. Instead the emancipatory method suppresses the two characters that are set up by the very dramaturgy of explanation: the *pais* and the *agōgos* (the guide). It says: there is no accredited guide because there is no right point of departure, no right order. The whole is everywhere: The book that is in your hands is a whole from which you can discover your own capacity of making an infinite number of connections, hence your capacity of making links and wholes in general. The only condition of those operations is an "opinion": the opinion of the equality of intelligence: the opinion that there is only one intelligence and that the master and the student are only two speaking beings, two travellers weaving their path in the forest of things and signs. From this we can deduce the second reason for which intellectual emancipation is not an alternative pedagogy or an anti-pedagogy: intellectual emancipation is not about teaching and learning. It is about equality and inequality. Or rather it is about teaching and learning only to the extent that their relationship embodies the logic of inequality. The social institution of intellectual inequality is not enclosed within the academic forms of transmission of knowledge. It is present all over the surface of human relationships, wherever the acts of speaking, writing, reading, listening or seeing take on the form of commanding and consenting, guiding and following, showing and perceiving, informing and being informed, and a multiplicity of similar relationships which frame the territory of our experience and draw the paths on which we can move over this territory.

What has to be unlearned thus is the logic of explanation. Now, there are two ways of understanding this "unlearning" which imply two different uses of the negation. The first one conceives the negation in the form of a "forget it." Leave it aside. Or move aside. This is the way in which Jacotot conceives of this un-learning: let the institution carry out the endless task of perfecting its perfected explanations; move aside, over the wide free space neglected by the explicators, in order to open the multiple ways of verifying the equality of intelligence; weave the thread of a community of equals beside the institutions of the inegalitarian society.

Unfortunately we have no more the possibility to think in those terms. We have not because, since his time, the principle of extensiveness and the principle of progressiveness have taken on new forms and combined with each other in new ways that have entirely mapped the vacant territories on which he proposed to find new ways of knowing "something" and relating to it all the rest. The reason for this is simple: all those vacant spaces have been integrated into the territory of knowledge. Such is the work that has been implemented by the infinite extension of a new science which was still in its childhood in Jacotot's time: social science. Social science has waged an endless war against ignorance and ignoramuses. It has invaded all the territories where science had heretofore disregarded to go. It found that in every part of those territories there was something worth knowing and it linked all those portions of knowledge in the knowledge of the global system. By the same token it made ignorance itself the object of an ever-increasing body of knowledge explaining why the ignoramuses were unable to know what was before them at hand.

For a long time, this infinite extension had been associated with a promise of equality: since the global connection was the connection of a system of domination, its knowledge was supposed to forge the weapons of liberation. Including the territories of misery, wildness and ignorance in the empire of science was the way of making science the weapon of a collective action which would erase misery, wildness and ignorance. The hitch was that this egalitarian project was itself entirely dependent upon the temporal logic of the system that it was destined to destroy: the logic of progressiveness, which means the logic of the inequality of intelligence, separating those who can understand the connections of the whole and those who are entrapped in the universe of the particular and all the more separated from their own experience as this experience has been entirely captured in the nets of science. In such a way the promise of equality, carried by social science, was ultimately absorbed by the inegalitarian logic. On the one side, it was overturned: the science of the global system of domination which was destined to provide the ways of destroying it became the science of its necessary reproduction. On the other side, the "equality" of social science came to be simply identified with the equal availability of any phenomenon to become an object of science. This is what can be called the cultural turn of social science. During the last decades, we have witnessed an incredible increase of research and writing dealing with all aspects of media culture, visual culture, popular cultural and minority cultures, as well as the engagement of many film and media scholars with the extensive study of high or low quality TV series, and the constant annexation to the territory of academic research of all forms of popular entertainment, youth culture, ethnic music, dress codes of all youth groups and sub-groups, and so on.

The introduction of all that material in academic research and teaching has readily been hailed as a recognition of the equal dignity of all producers and consumers of cultural practices. Against the old aristocratic definition of culture, the new cultural studies have affirmed that "there is no outside to culture." During this conference on "unlearning" Jack Halberstam and Paul Bowman have eloquently shown what we can learn from the operations of thought and art that are at work everywhere.[1] But there is the flip side of the coin. The inclusion of

---

1   See below Paul Bowman's "The Intimate Schoolmaster and the Ignorant *Sifu*: Bruce Lee and the Ignorance of Everyday Radical Pedagogy," Chapter 5. Jack

all social practices in the empire of science also is a form of dispossession: science grabs hold of any form of occupation or entertainment of the ordinary people to make them its objects. The "no outside to culture" thus proclaims that, since there is no hierarchy, nothing and nobody will eschew the grip of science.

There is no space left outside science. This new extension of the principle of extensiveness ties up with the new progress of the principle of progressiveness: there is no time outside science. This connection is best epitomized by the form of "popular knowledge" that has expanded at the same rhythm as the academic development of social science, namely journalism. Yesteryear journalism was accused either of lying or of sticking to the surface of things. Contemporary media are accused of drowning us in an ocean of news and images that we are unable to master. I think that both accusations are beside the point. The "so-called" banality of the newspaper is nothing else than the popularization of the explications of social science which precisely turn the chronicle of the everyday into the connections of scientific knowledge. And the media don't drown us in an ocean of images. On the contrary they select them and reduce them to the mere illustration of their meaning, as it is "explained," hour by hour, by experts in sociology, political science and so on. Their function is to create consensus, which means the perfect correspondence between sense and sense, i.e., between the perceptible and the thinkable. It is to produce and reproduce this correspondence without any interruption, to match up at any time any event with its explication. In such a way, the knowledge of society comes to be coextensive with the life of society, and the demonstration of this correspondence occupies the entire time of each day. This ceaseless demonstration of correspondence is at the same time a twofold demonstration of inequality. On the one hand, it continuously reproduces the

[*cont.*] Halberstam's "A Path So Twisted: Thinking Wildly With and Through Punk Feminisms" was also delivered at *The Pedagogics of Unlearning* conference at Trinity College Dublin on September 7, 2014. See the conference website www.unlearningconf.com for all abstracts, audio and YouTube downloads of these papers. — Ed.

distance between the common people who undergo the events that are told by the media (the victims of war, violence, natural disasters, economic collapses, de-industrialization, etc.) and the experts who can explain them. On the other hand, it ceaselessly reproduces the ignorance of the readers, spectators or listeners who are shown at every moment that they would not understand the most prosaic events if they were not given explications by the experts who alone can decipher the signification which is ciphered in any of them. This is how the two principles get increasingly tied in with each other: the co-extensiveness of science and society is presented in a temporal form that equates it with the ceaseless reproduction of inequality. In such a way the logic of explanation saturates the whole field of experience. The pedagogical order now covers the whole of the social fabric. Not only do the teachers and the textbooks explain; all our institutions, our governments, the myriad of committees and subcommittees that they create, the intellectuals, the experts and the media are all committed to the task of endlessly explaining everything, from the hard constraints of the global market to the deep trends revealed by the last opinion polls or the civilization crisis witnessed by the most trivial events. In such a way the reasons of power are increasingly equated with the reasons of science, which means that any resistance to those reasons becomes a manifestation of ignorance. At the end of the day, the social order is simply equated with the inequality of intelligence.

The logic of explanation is thus much more than a matter of schooling and pedagogy. It is a time-machine producing at the same rhythm an imaginary concordance and an actual discordance of times. Let us think of the process of harmonization of European diplomas known as the Bologna process. This harmonization does much more than create an equivalence between diplomas; it constructs an ideal uniformity of degree courses, so that the time spent to get those degrees signify the knowledge that has been acquired. This equivalence thus becomes part of a dreamed harmony between the time of the global economic process and the lived time of the individuals through the adjustment between the skills that have been acquired and the job opportunities resulting from their adaptation to the forms of economic development. The hitch is that the job opportunities are not so much determined by the progress of science and technology as they are by the play of financial speculation. But this is precisely the way in which the play of concordance and discordance, success and failure reaches its perfection. On the one hand, the less the reality of the market verifies the concordance of times, the more the educational institutions must embody the fiction of that concordance. If they cannot open the gates of the business world to their students, they must at least work as private companies submitted to the rules of good management: the universities and the research teams are invited to merge like companies in order to weigh more in the Shanghai ranking and they get funds if they follow research programs that bureaucratic committees select as key themes, destined to perfect the perfect harmony between scientific research and economic prosperity. Of course this harmony is indefinitely delayed. The time of the educational institutions never catches up with the time of the global economy. But the main function of the machine of concordance is precisely to reproduce indefinitely a discordance that the actors of the system — students, professors, researchers — must experience as their own failure and the endless demonstration of their incapacity to fulfil a promise which is no more a promise of equality but a mere promise of adaptation, a mere promise of correspondence with one's own time.

The explanatory system then appears as a principle of saturation which inscribes the presupposition of inequality in all the forms of exercise of intellectual activity. It is no more an affair of pedagogy and of pedagogical relationship. On the one hand, the explanatory logic of the educational system now rests on the bureaucratic programming of the concordance and discordance of temporalities much more than it does on the forms of transmission of knowledge. On the other hand, it is present everywhere in the framing of the perceptible, the set of relationships between the perceptible and its meaning and the modes of causal linkage at work in the most trivial news bulletin as well as in the definition and the distribution of the academic disciplines that have caught everybody and everything in the nets of social knowledge. If it is so, the negative operation of "un-learning" can no more be thought of as a "forget it," as the exploration of the vacant spaces outside the academic system. Instead it is an operation that takes place inside the fabric of explanation which covers the whole territory of experience, an operation that unties the threads that the explanatory logic has weaved between the facts and their knowledge, the things and their meanings, the images and the words, the events and their causes. It is a matter of un-explaining.

Un-explaining in general means undoing the opinion of inequality. Undoing it means undoing the links that it has tightened everywhere between the perceptible and the thinkable. On the one hand, the un-explanatory method unties the stitches of the veil that the explanatory system has spread on everything; it restores the things that this system caught in its nets to their singularity and makes them available to the perception and the intelligence of anybody. On the other hand it returns their opacity, their lack of evidence, to the modes of presentation and argumentation which were supposed to cast light on them. By so doing it substitutes a community of equal speaking beings for the distribution of the positions opposing the learned to the ignoramuses. This operation in turn implies that we question the very relation between the subjects of knowledge and its objects. I wish to focus, through a few examples, on some specific procedures of un-explanation working at some strategic points of articulation in order to undo the explanatory modes of presentation of things and production of meaning which inscribe inequality in the consensual landscape of the perceptible and the thinkable.

I will start with the simplest of the categories through which explanation works and through which it can be undone, namely the category of quantity. I recalled earlier that journalistic practice rested on a specific operation: selection. The selection of a few significant features is destined to put order in the confusion of the multiple which means two things: the confusion of the events that must be given a single meaning and the confusion of the multitudes to which those events happen in disorder. As a matter of fact, the operation is a bit more complicated since the selection has a twofold aspect. On the one hand, the confusion of the multiple must be shown as the landscape of the "real" that has been visited by the reporter: the landscape in which the men and women of the multitude live those events in their particularity. On the other hand, the journalist must select in the décor of the multiple the few significant features which make sense of it by integrating them into a pre-existing interpretive grid. The practice of reportage is thus a certain arrangement of perceptual facts and of significations usually associated with those facts; it is a certain set of relations between the individual and the whole, between the markers of individual reality and the signifiers of statistical generality. It is that combination of the particular and the general, of facts and meanings, images and words that must be dismantled by the operation of un-explanation. The best example of such a practice was given by the extravagant reportage made by James Agee and Walker Evans in 1936 among the Alabama sharecroppers. Each of them took up the part of the other and did the contrary of what was expected from him. The photographer did not provide the spectacle of this hotchpotch of dirty things and persons which is the usual landscape of misery. On the contrary, he showed an insignificant décor of order and scarcity: a section of wall in planks with small boards nailed askew and tinplate cutlery and utensils supported by cross-beams; the corner of a room with a piece of rag on a cloth line between a straw-bottomed chair and a broom; a well-arranged dining room seen from the corridor with a washbowl in the foreground; the members of a family posing as they would do it in an ordinary photographer's studio. On his part, Agee refused to select in the décor of the destitute sharecroppers the marks and signs that would have made their lives available for the consumption of the readers. He played the part of the photographer by making a multiplicity of close-ups which turned any prosaic object or kitsch chromo into a relic encapsulating the whole sense of a destiny. His inventory of all the items stored in all the drawers of the house, his attempt at capturing the light or the smell of the oil lamp, the grain and the scent of the pine planks of the walls and the breath of the sleeping bodies, his description of the innumerable patches that make the overall of the sharecropper look "as intricate and fragile as the feather mantle of a Toltec prince" pushed to the extreme the "democracy" — the impossibility of selecting — of which literature, since Flaubert's time, had been accused. Its exhaustive enumeration undid the consensual relationship between the whole and the fragment, the general and the particular. Instead it connected those lives with the infinity of the connections in space and time contained in a single minute of the world, with that inexhaustible totality of every instant that literature, in the age of Proust and Virginia Woolf, had opposed to the journalistic selection of marks and signs which frames consensus.

This practice of dis-proportion thus opens out onto a wider dismantlement of other categories set to work in the operations that inscribe inequality in the landscape of knowledge, notably the categories of relation and modality. I am thinking here of the operations that I was obliged to perform myself in order to account for the operations performed in some 19th-century workers' letters and diaries that chance once put into my hands: the letters exchanged by friends telling the timetable of a day in the Saint-Simonian community or the Sunday walk of three workers exchanging metaphysical hypotheses in country inns; the letters of a joiner inviting a cesspool cleaner to leave his degrading job and the answers of the cesspool cleaner celebrating this night job which allowed him to enjoy freedom during the day; the diaries of the same joiner narrating, hour by hour, the day at work in a factory or the day at work as a floor-layer in a private house. In the usual framework of social science such letters or diaries are perceived as chronicles of the everyday, expressing the way in which individual workers could perceive and express a situation which was itself part of a whole set of historical transformations of industrial capitalism. They are the documentary material that science has to explain by showing the causes that made them possible. I was lucky enough to vaguely perceive that those diaries were not chronicles of the everyday. Instead, they were intellectual exercises transforming the very way of living the everyday and the very modality of its description. They were part of a whole set of intellectual and physical exercises destined to break the very opposition between the two modes of temporality opposed by Aristotle's *Poetics*: the time of mere succession allotted to those who live in the everyday, and the rational plot linking the causes and effects of action and knowledge according to necessity or verisimilitude. By the same token, they broke the platonic distribution of times which destined the workers to limit themselves to the exercise of the aptitudes given to them by the god because "work does not wait." Those exercises worked thus at the very point of articulation which inscribes the inequality of intelligence into the division of times. At this point the "objects" of science changed their modal status by affirming themselves as speaking beings. They were no more the fragments of a whole that had to be explained, they were making a whole themselves, reconstructing a world of experience.

If it was so, the discourse destined to account for that change had to change its own modality. It could no more be a discourse explaining those writings by locating them in the whole of the connections that made them *possible*. It had to start from their reality of intellectual operations, reconfiguring a whole world of experience. It could not be the discourse of a definite specialist of social science, be it the historian, the sociologist, or the philosopher. Not only must this discourse erase the boundaries which annul the equality of the speaking beings in the division of the objects and territories of science, it also has to erase the very difference between the modality of a discourse and the modality of its "object." It must erase the hierarchical privilege of the comment whose words explain the words that are its "object." But it must also avoid the pretention to leave the other, the native or the subaltern, speak in his/her "own" language — which can be the most efficient way of reinforcing the old hierarchy separating those whose voices express their pleasure or their pain and those who can spell out the reasons of pleasure and pain. The only solution was to allow the voices to penetrate into each other, which meant annulling the difference between the narration of the facts and the comment which explains it.

This is how I adopted this theoretical form that I chose long after to call the scene. The scene sets to work, in its own way, the principle that "everything is in everything." It describes an event which is more than an event; an event which at the same time shows us the border between the event and the non-event, between what is ordinary and what is not, what has its place in a given order of signification and what is out or in-between. If we want to describe the content of the scenes on which I focused, we can say that they are scenes of metamorphosis: they stage the process through which a life affirms its capacity of being an object of thought for itself. This content imposes a specific form. It obliges to break the border separating theory from profane experience in order to show how the whole of the theoretical question is at work in those little stories. The scene is the mode of presentation in which the very difference between the words and sentences of knowledge and the words and sentences of those who are its "objects" is suppressed. Both appear to belong to the same language and to the same capacity of thinking. There is not a language for empirical narration and a language for theoretical explanation. There is one language and one intelligence. To deliver its energetic potential the scene needs no explanation. It only needs intensification. Its capacity of making things perceptible and thinkable has to be intensified by making the scenes resonate and be mirrored into one another. Proust once told us that we should use his book as a lens through which we look into our own life and experience. The scene can be viewed as a little optical machine allowing us to look into the other scenes and make what is at issue in them appear in the foreground. But it is not only a question of better sight. It is also a question of liberating the subversive energy encapsulated in those scenes, the energy of the crossing of the border.

It can be said to be a matter of art. But we must understand "art" here in the Jacototian way: as an egalitarian practice of research annulling the separation between the ignoramus and the learned. More precisely, we can think of an art of equality which works as a counter-method, reconfiguring the ways in which people, things and events are put together, according to the dominant rules of articulation between the perceptible and the thinkable. A community of equals, just as a community of unequal people is first framed through the way in which facts and meanings get into a community: in the construction of a sentence, the narration of an event, the argument about its meaning, the comment on an image, the mode of existence of a character on a stage or a screen, etc. From that point of view the extravagant inventory through which Agee undid the very relationship between the one and the multiple, the particular and the general, or the construction of the sentences in which I made my voice indiscernible from Jacotot's voice or from the voice of the joiner, Gauny, belong to the same logic of redistribution of the positions that I analyzed in various contemporary artworks. I am thinking, for instance, of the way in which Alfredo Jaar redistributes at the same time the relations between the one and the multiple and the relations between the words and the images when he installs in the space of an exhibition a series of names, the image of a single look and a narration or a pile of slides of that single look in the place of the piles of massacred bodies which were expected (Rancière 2008). I am also thinking of the way in which Pedro Costa erases the boundary between fiction and documentary — which actually is a distinction between two kinds of human beings — when, by the play of some almost imperceptible displacements in the gestures and the tones of his characters, he allows two immigrant workers to move from the status of documentary bodies witnessing a condition to the status of artistic subjects restaging that condition as their own story in a series of short scenes.

I tried to give some examples of un-explanatory operations. We must not, however, be mistaken about the meaning of the word "operation." Not incidentally did I speak, in my own case, of chance and of vague perception. As a matter of fact, none of the operations that I have just spelled out was ever planned. It was produced by the constraint of the "material" itself, that is, by the constraint of the emancipatory operations performed by the texts which were my "material." It was a way of reacting to a surprise or taking up a challenge; a way of learning, as an ignoramus, from texts which had certainly never been destined to teach me anything. What I learned was not something destined to be taught: I learnt first to construct, by groping along in the dark, a new way of perceiving and telling. "Un-learning" can also mean this: the dissociation between the acts of teaching and learning; the fact that you learn from somebody or something that never taught you. This means in turn that you don't teach what you have learnt. You can just tell it, invent a manner of telling it out of which possibly others will learn from you something else, something that you don't know.

This might be the deepest meaning — which also means the deepest challenge — of the "un" present in "unlearning" and "un-explaining." In a sense, there is something wrong with this negative prefix. The un-explanation is not a negative form of criticism. It is not a denunciation of the explicative practice. It is an entirely positive practice, which tries to weave a sensorium of equality, erasing the barriers that the explicative system had put on the paths of the communication between speaking beings. This is how I tried to practice a mode of writing by way of which the intellectual exercises of the researcher, the intellectual exercises of those who were his "objects," the intellectual exercises of antique philosophers and those of modern sociologists were given the same mode of existence, the same status as performances of speaking beings telling their intellectual adventures. But the positive weaving of this fabric of intellectual equality can only be done by producing gaps in the normal complementarity of intellectual operations: searching, learning, knowing, and teaching. The "un" of unlearning or unexplaining does not simply mean that we break with the normal forms of teaching and learning. It points to a dissymmetry — or a dissociation — at the heart of those forms. We learn as ignoramuses and we teach as ignoramuses. We learn something from people who never taught us anything. We don't teach what we have learnt. We teach without knowing what we teach. The normal complementarity of those operations has been absorbed by the intensification of the first term of the chain: searching.

Two consequences must be drawn from this. The first one is that the distance between the practices of intellectual equality and the logic of the explicative institutions is irreducible. This irreducibility cannot be equated with the distinction made by Jacotot between the individual act of emancipation and the collective working of social institutions. The main point is not about individuals and collectives (which means, in passing, that intellectual emancipation is not, as some "critical" minds have it, a theory of the neo-liberal subject). The difference concerns the very structure of the intellectual operations and the mode of their linkage. The gap separating learning, knowing, and teaching is a gap between temporalities. This gap disrupts the temporal logic of the explicative institutions which presupposes the homogeneity of the temporal process of learning, the better to trace inside it the dividing line of inequality. The intellectual operations which weave the sensorium of intellectual equality can never coincide with those which contribute to the functioning of the explicative machine. By saying this, I am not taking up the mournful critical discourse which affirms that, in spite of their good intentions, the members of the educative institutions can do nothing but reproduce a system of domination. Instead, I wish to emphasize that it is always possible to create forms of manifestation of intellectual equality in the places that are destined to the functioning of the explicative logic. But the creation of such possibilities can never coincide with a revolution of the logic of the institution. The time of the institution is determined by the anticipation of the effects of the learning process. As I mentioned earlier, this planning and this anticipation may become and often becomes a lie. But the institution cannot live without them. And this is precisely what the logic of intellectual equality forbids: the success of its operations depends upon encounters that may happen or not happen. Those encounters produce unpredictable effects in spaces of time which cannot be anticipated. They can happen inside the explicative institution, but their time cannot coincide with its time. This is the crucial point which has been missed in the attempts to change the "pedagogical relation." My generation has known some moments of revolutionary effervescence when it was proclaimed that the professors would not teach anymore and that open discussion would be substituted for authoritarian lecturing. All this resulted in a quick return to the old order. It did so because the distribution of academic positions rests on something more radical: a distribution of temporalities. This is why there is no counter-institution inverting the logic of the institution. Un-explanation is not symmetric to explanation. It cannot build an alternative time-machine, because its temporality does not allow an anticipation of the effects.

There is no un-explicative institution. But there are a multiplicity of practices, inside or outside the dominant institutions, which extend the community of equal speaking beings and open new paths for the circulation of thought, new forms of access to research and knowledge. This is a slow time indeed. But this slow time of subversion of the explicative logic can find its resonance in other forms of disruption of the dominant temporality. I am thinking of those moments of interruption which recently happened in the streets and squares of many cities when unexpected crowds of anonymous persons, responding to calls made through the social networks and not by the self-proclaimed political groups, gathered without specific claims, just to affirm their refusal of the way in which the spaces and times of our lives are managed by the alliance of state powers and financial oligarchies. At this point, I think that the logic of un-explanation can meet with the logic of occupation. An occupation is a form of relationship between a distribution of spaces and times and the exercise of a capacity. Now, this relationship can take on two antagonistic forms. There is the police notion of occupation that I analyzed in *The Philosopher and his Poor* when commenting on Plato's statement about the necessity for the artisans to stay all the time in their workshop and do only their own business for two reasons that make a circle: firstly, work does not wait; secondly, the god has given them the aptitude fitting this job and none other (Rancière 2004). That logic of occupation was overturned in modern times when the workers occupied their factories and, by so doing, affirmed at once their power over the space and time of their work and their intellectual capacity. In the 1960s, the occupation of the universities by the students was intended to stop the machine of production and reproduction of the social hierarchy. Occupation thus is a political form of un-explanation, undoing the knot which links a distribution of spaces and times with a distribution of capacities. In a time when factories are closed and industry relocated, it plays this role in a different way: it becomes a way of reconstructing a common space and a common temporality for individuals that the logic of domination has scattered into a multiplicity of fragmented times and spaces — a reconstruction which entails the experimentation of new uses of time and new exercises of intellectual capacity.

It is true that those forms of un-explanation have often been seen as ephemeral interruptions unable to change anything in the dominant order because of their lack of strategy. I think that it is possible to turn this argument on its head: this kind of criticism belongs itself to the logic of explanation, the logic that expects equality to come as a result of the development of time, society, and knowledge. Instead, the so-called "ephemeral" movements implement the logic of "everything is in everything": the whole of the logic of equality and inequality, the whole of their conflict is present everywhere at every moment. And the history of the last two centuries shows us that the possibility of new worlds had only been made thinkable out of some episodes of a few days during which the normal course of time — the normal distribution of times and capabilities — had been broken, and ordinary men and women had verified the equality of intelligences by setting to work unexpected capabilities.

I will conclude by comparing two stories of "unlearning" dealing precisely with time. In his *Theses on the Concept of History,* Benjamin took up an anecdote about the 1830 Revolution in Paris: the story of a man who shot at the clocks to stop time just as Joshua stopped the sun in the Bible (Benjamin 2007, 261–62). Benjamin put it in the context of his idea of messianic time. It is clear, however, that the story had been forged by learned people eager to show the stupidity of the rioting mob and the utopian dreamers. For my part, I prefer another story of stupidity that is another story of "unlearning time." One of the landmarks of the occupation of Gezi Park in Istanbul was the performance of the "standing man," for more than five hours, he stood still and silent, with his hands in his pockets, staring at the portrait of Atatürk on the façade of the Atatürk Cultural Center. Other persons gathered around him in the same attitude, putting in a predicament the police that were not used to this form of subversion. This way of breaking through time was in keeping with a collective action about the very use of a space, an action aimed at preserving the indeterminacy of a place, keeping it available for sitting, walking, discussing, or just doing nothing, whereas the power wanted to create there two "useful" places: a military building and a shopping mall. The "stupidity" of the standing man symbolizes the creation of a space of experimentation of new uses of time and new demonstrations of equal capability, ranging from the organization of daily life in the street to the discussion about the meaning of the movement. This is why I think that this performance can also provide us with a good image of what un-explaining can mean as both an entirely negative and an entirely positive process.

REFERENCES

Aristotle. *Poetics*, ed. S. H. Butcher. Devon: Dover Publications.
Benjamin, W. (2007). "Theses on the Philosophy of History," in *Illuminations: Essays and Reflections*, trans. Harry Zohn and ed. Hannah Arendt. New York: Schocken Books.
Rancière, J. (1991). *The Ignorant Schoolmaster: Five Lessons in Intellectual Emancipation*, trans. Kristin Ross. Stanford: Stanford University Press.
———. (2004). *The Philosopher and His Poor*, trans. John Drury et al. and ed. Andrew Parker. Durham and London: Duke University Press.

———. (2008). "Theatre of Images," in *Alfredo Jaar: The Politics of Images.* Zurich: JRP|Ringier.

2

Phantasies of the Writing Block: A Psychoanalytic Contribution to Pernicious Unlearning[1]

Deborah Britzman

A Note to the Reader

By way of background, the notion of "unlearning" has a strong history of critique in the field of public education, first tied to Kantian Enlightenment with the overturning of self-induced forms of immaturity, and then the failure of Enlightenment. The movement here has been from the desire for knowledge to not wanting knowledge at all. Contemporary discussions on the complex of unlearning emerge from post-war thought: for example, within Adorno's essay "Education after Auschwitz," and within the postcolonial theory of Fanon's *Black Skin, White Masks* and Freire's *Pedagogy of the Oppressed*, and also feminist pedagogy's consciousness-raising procedures and queer

---

1 This contribution is a shortened variation of a chapter in D. Britzman's (2015) *A Psychoanalyst in the Classroom: On the Human Condition of Education* (Albany: State University of New York Press).

pedagogy's deconstruction of normalcy. By the early 1970s, "unlearning racism, sexism, and homophobia" became a structural feature of curriculum in university classrooms. With critical pedagogy, the turn was to ideological critique and knowledge of the mechanisms of social inequality, thereby inciting a proliferation of pedagogical orientations for liberation. Problems ensued, however, with the question of pedagogy and, with the emphasis on reading and writing, literary theorists such as Shoshanna Felman, Barbara Johnson, and Eve Kosofsky Sedgwick rewrote the question of learning with Lacanian, Kleinian, and Freudian theories that considered the status of the unconscious and symptoms of learning and not learning. It is here that knowledge and ignorance became a fraught couple. I considered many of these uneven developments — the foremost is with the mismatch between teaching and learning — in my earlier book, *Novel Education: Psychoanalytic Studies of Learning and not Learning* (New York: Peter Lang Press, 2006).

The current paper had a long gestation. It began many years ago with a note to myself: "Write about the writing block." I listed a few short stories and novels as touchstones and over the years became quite surprised at the sheer amount of literature that in some way leaned upon expressions of writing inhibitions. The untold story of the writing block thus became the never-ending story. There is a bit of irony in the present project since one of the features of both the never-ending story and the writing block is that they must remain unfinished and incomplete and so cannot know duration.

In my current communication I can now turn to the writing block as opening a particular configuration of the difficulty of unlearning the repetition compulsion, itself a quality of writing, the drive/object dilemma, and a means for its working through. Thus from the vantage of the emotional situation of the writing block I explore a psychoanalytic reconsideration of pernicious unlearning. My hunch is that people come to the university to experience their writing inhibitions. I first ask why reading for anxiety matters for understanding what happens affectively while trying to write. This will take us into more discussion on manifest and latent anxiety through examples from writers and psychoanalysts who articulate and disperse their feelings about writing as they write. From there, I trace a third path, with the idea that one can write one's way into and out of anxiety provided that the dynamics of writing can be linked to a constellation of libidinal conflicts that bring to the fore matters of loyalty, affiliation, ideality, separation, and finding one's own way.

Once Again, But This Time with Feeling

> *It gives you a queer feeling if late in life, you are ordered once again to write a school essay.* […] *It is strange how readily you obey the orders, as though nothing in particular had happened in the last half century.*
> — Sigmund Freud, "Some Reflections on a Schoolboy Psychology"

Freud's (1914) ode to shrinking education tarries with the unconscious. Word by word his reverie sounds the sotto voce of writing and releases the feel of a dream: *queer feelings, late, orders, once again, school, strange, obey, nothing happened, and you.* Yes, the rule of the school essay is replete with writing's transpositions; it animates our capacity for decomposition and leaves us pleading for more time. Let us try to listen for the writer's subjunctive mood — be that as it may — to ask, what rules the order to write and what, in writing, does the writer both obey and defy "*once again*"? Throughout my discussion, I stay close to the clinical construction that words arouse anxiety and libido. Thus refined writing becomes: between the lines the writer pens the force of her or his emotional situation along with the wish to risk that fate and to create something new from more than what has already happened.

Recall that a sixty-year-old Freud (1914) was given a late assignment from teachers no longer and that he used the occasion to notice the transference torrents of his childhood education made from his wishes to both know and please his teachers. But he cannot do that again, and the essay's title, "Reflections on a Schoolboy Psychology," overwrites that loss. Writing anxiety has a tenuous foothold in that conflicted desire to please and to influence, though the pathos of the writing block mainly belongs to the adult. It is then that the desire to please and influence are at odds, and gradually each side of the conflict takes on greater ambitions along with their dangers: social anxiety (whether others hate the writing), moral anxiety (whether the writing destroys a law or must protect it), and ego-anxiety (whether it is the self that must lose respect). For the psychoanalyst in the classroom the writing block reassembles the human condition of separation, thought of as a constellation of phantasies, anxieties, and defenses that plot the loss of experience, the other, the self, the idea, the teacher, the group, the career, etc. If such emotional binds were the end of the story, we would need to do nothing more. But this unconscious history of separation and union surprise the writer with a new demand: read for where anxiety and its phantasy delegates irrupt in order to write before them.

Yet there is discontentment with the attempt to communicate what happens for the writer. In trying to convey the untold story of a writing block, I find myself caught in its decompositions, its exorbitant retellings, its repetitive style, and the acting out. While writing this paper, I lost my interest, felt no one cared, was sure someone else had already written it, and gave up hope that the disparate pieces of thought would take me any further than a description of what everyone already knows. Draft upon draft drove me into more muddles. I lost my train of thought and felt out of focus. Suddenly, I needed to read more. Then I began to hate writing. It was making me suffer. In these symptomatic acts I am both culprit and innocent, both omnipotent and helpless. And if this transference to the writing block rather than with communicating the writing of it is a part of the writer's neurosis, we now have a bare clue that it is quite possible to write without knowing one is blocked. Resistance is an astounding quality of its untold history. But so too is otherness that belongs to the creativity of primary processes and the force of the drives that Georg Groddeck proposed early on as "the compulsion to symbolize" (cited in M'Uzan 2013, 10).

My main approach is to pass the act of writing through to its constellations of phantasies — the emotional logic, dramatic personae and delegates, object relations, and sequelae of psychical events that animate as well as deaden one's style. Because the writer has to rely upon the self who in turn must associate with words and ideas in the making, writing is also a means to create a self who writes. While such an observation sounds obvious, the self is oblivious. The writer's dilemma involves the problem of learning to read anxiety's delegates, by which I mean attending to the often maddening phantasies, defenses, and neurotic solutions that split off the writer from the writing and render the act and the actor as meaningless. The work is to analyze the power and dispersal of unconscious conflicts that, more often than not, divide passion into warring factions of love and hate and tear the writer into bits and pieces. Whether anxiety opts for the paragraph, sentence, or word, a story is being written and it is in writing that one may transform the writing phantasy into a commentary on problems in the wider world. The paradox is that conflicted psychical life and the obstacles, terror, object relations, and desire carried into the world of others remains our first resource for disquieting imagination. Writing, after all, involves the intermingling of reality and phantasy.

So I bring for your consideration a few intertwining dilemmas, best posed as questions. How may the writer be in communication with what is most abstract or unconscious in the affecting psychodynamics of writing? And, drawing from Melanie Klein ([1952] 1975), how may the writer come "to acknowledge the increasingly poignant psychic reality" (73) so easily denied? However strange it is to imagine that when we tear up the page, the self too feels in bits and pieces, it is in writing that we have access to the emotional situations we have faced before and that return again as omnipotent phantasy that defends against infantile helplessness and dependency on the good object that might suddenly turn bad. We owe this formulation to Klein's insistence on a sort of prehistoric emotional situation made from the infant's earliest defenses of introjection, splitting, projection, and identification that she called the schizoid mechanisms of object relations. Anxiety, she maintained is the bare capacity for symbolization as much as it is the road to inhibitions.

Klein ([1946] 1975) also proposed the estranging term "latent anxiety" to consider an unconscious sequence of phantasy events that suggests deferral and defense. One may be in the throes of anxiety but not know that affect has meaning, contingencies, origins, or effects. Defenses against persecutory feelings are being made and emptied of recognition. The latency occurs, she writes, "by the particular method of dispersal. The feeling of being disintegrated, of being unable to experience emotions, of losing one's objects, is in fact the equivalent of anxiety" (21). As with the dream work, a sequence of anxiety unfolds: fragmentation, projection, loss, destruction, and displacement. Not knowing and needing to know brings the frustrated writer to feel wrong but unable to question the problem. Then comes a second dilemma: the writing block being written resists its own telling, and this latency is an unusual claim given how often we complain about not being able to write the way we want and not knowing what holds us back. The writing may be going well and then, just as suddenly, is treated as worthless. Hard to say what has happened. But it feels as if the love affair has gone wrong.

There is plenty of frustration to pass around and displacement serves that function, but the sequence of anxiety begins with an unbearable aggression. For Klein, the earliest problem is libidinal and already symbolic in that libido seeks objects. Aggression, perhaps the earliest response to drive frustration and itself a sign of life, begins with introjection or taking inside parts of the external world only to worry that the act of incorporation, like eating, devastates the integrity of the object who seems to know it is being destroyed. The object turns to shit and so must be evacuated. Then come worries that the object is angry and will return to destroy us. Yet even in this fight to the finish, something new occurs: within the anguish of the paranoid–schizoid position, new doubts and concerns for the object occur through a mental constellation Klein named the depressive position, a concern for the object relation, however imaginary. The ego or self is at odds with the mix-up of desire and frustration as it confronts the emotional situation or psychical reality of the destruction and reparation of the good object. Writing, it seems, oscillates between these two anxieties.

The numerous anxiety situations Klein ([1935] 1975) identified as our earliest emotional situation and that serve as an obsessive index of loss may be read as a good enough allegory for what the writer then faces:

> To quote only a few of them: there is anxiety how to put the bits together in the right way and at the right time; how to pick out the good bits and do away with the bad ones; how to bring the object to life when it has been put together; and there is the anxiety of being interfered with in this task by bad objects and by one's own hatred, etc. (269)

Bad objects become bad thoughts, and all this is hated because they were once good objects and loved. Our double attitude of love and hate leads Klein to her most difficult existential contention: the basis of anxiety is the hatred of psychical life that is itself a phantasy further agonized by the defense of denial of psychical reality. Klein maintains that fear of destruction, what she saw as the death drive, forms the bottomlessness of depression and the painful latency at work in the defence of inhibition.

While there is always more than one story, the situation of the writing block contains common subjective elements: unhappiness, frustration, depression, neurosis, obsessionality, and separation anxiety. Emotional consternation tends to be split off from experience and placed under the sign "nothing happens." Ironically, the writing block presents in voluntary settings dependent upon the social bond, such as university, psychoanalytic institutes, academic journals, conferences, dissertations, and various assignments that call upon the ego's desire to write and the superego's dedicated hostility. In writing, anxiety and desire go hand in hand. The odd part is that one comes to the university as either a professor or a student to write, and may find the self now driving around in the state of a writing block. And it is a guilty state ordered by rules, rituals, and courts of law. There are writing police, stop signs, go directly to jail cards, waiting in line, traffic jams, accidents, expired permits, and assurance policies. The writing block is a character world of object relations, many of whom are suspicious of the desire to write. "Who cares?" the poor writer thinks to no one in particular.

Even in nomenclature the writing block repeats its conflictive designs. No one is there. In the name of nothing there can be little agreement as to etiology, precipitating factors, genetic evolution, symptomology, causality, and so, subjective predicament. Except for the gigantic disappointment factor, the writing block is hard to read. A psychoanalyst named Edmund Bergler coined the term in his 1947 paper "Further Contributions to the Psychoanalysis of Writers." While his nickname, the writing block, has great legs, the paper is largely forgotten, not only because it contains a riot of opinion or that it reads as a self-parody of mid-century psychoanalysis and its preoccupation with the analyst as all-knowing figurehead. Bergler's dusty work is ignored because he can't help hating the writer in trouble, and readers do receive that hostility. His view is that the writing block is a regression into the oral-cannibalistic phase of libido that leans upon infantile defenses that fend off persecutory anxiety with the weapons of greed and envy. I do think that self-hatred is a complicated affair, but due to the fate that objects are always involved, in my view, Bergler's explanation repeats the problem by ignoring the suffering writer and why the writer feels at a loss. A few years later, Bergler (1950) wrote another defense of his theory, "Does 'Writer's block' exist?" He answers with certainty and concludes that anyone who cannot agree with him is stupid. Avital Ronell (2003), who wrote a book on stupidity, would have a field day. She insists, "Stupidity sets the mood that afflicts anyone who presumes to write" (24), and although she does not mention the famous block because it is not one stupid thing, she does rehearse a long list of flouncing affects the writer calls upon: depression, isolation, hostility, revenge phantasies, ambivalence, and anxiety.

Ronell admits that "a writer rarely confides the mood in which an act of writing is established" (2003, 63). She was discussing her invitation to a conference presentation where she was given a topic. For all kinds of reasons she accepted the assignment but then felt constrained by it and angry with herself. If everyone, she suggests, "has had the experience of writing in unfreedom," she continues this thought by characterizing writing as being "about the difficult hinge where the mirage of freedom and stark unfreedom meet" (64). And she then notes: "A wave of anxiety emerged with the work at hand" (64). There are, most of us will admit, pressures the writing sustains, and whether we call it our mood or simply our emotional situation, we do have to break free from something we may not know. Klein ([1946] 1975) considered such experiences of loss as interlinked to "the feeling of loneliness and the fear of parting" (13).

Roland Barthes' provocative lectures, *The Preparation of the Novel*, also picture writing from the side of its emotional situation: writing brings the writer to new realms of difficulties and pleasures (Barthes, 2011). The lectures concerned the phantasy of preparation and its disappearance. Barthes did not want to write a novel and seemed to enjoy the rumors that he was either busy at work or could not finish. Preparation has that quality: we have to imagine what goes into words and then disappears in writing. Barthes' pedagogical principle for his lectures was simply stated: "I sincerely believe that at the origin of teaching such as this we must always locate a fantasy, which can vary from year to year [...] The principle is a general one: the subject is not to be repressed — whatever the risks of subjectivity" (3). The risks belong to that which captures the writer but may also hold her back. He proposes a few solutions, such as taking drugs or even writing about the breakdown as many writers have done. The neurotic solution, Barthes councils, is to embrace and symbolize the neurosis:

> It's possible to imagine, as a solution, a sort of neurotic stratagem or plasticity: depending on the nature of the problem or of the breakdown, you exploit the different neuroses within yourself; for example, breakdowns at the outset: defeating the page, coming up with ideas, provoking the *spurt,* etc. = hys-

> terical activity ≠ the phase of Style, of Making Corrections, of Protection = obsessional activity. (269)

Barthes' ode to obsessional neurosis, however, because it is symbolized, creates a transitional space. I understand him as asking that we attempt to create from the movement of projective identification with melancholic object and to "identification of what doesn't work" (270). One can say that Barthes provides a creative writer position: "You exploit the different neurosis within yourself" (Barthes, ibid.). Then, one is forced to consider neurosis as having something to do with one's desire for symbolic freedom.

It seems to me that we can find the work of disquieting imagination in the writing incidents of psychoanalysts, novelists, and professors. That in turning to what they have to say we can entertain our obscurity and try to clear a pathway for symbolization. Psychoanalysts, novelists, and professors all write about not being able to write, about their endless preparation to write, and the difficulty of reading their own words and feeling estranged. The literature of the subjunctive mood involves subjective freedom and its disappearance. Between these poles I find a creative approach to analyzing or taking apart the old conflicts that make their way into the so-called writing block. Except for holding to Barthes' idea that we exploit the neurosis, I shall try to set aside an avalanche of advice and technologies of pedagogy that purport to cure the block, partly because writing already involves directions one cannot follow and partly because of my claim that the indefinite character of a writing block means that the writer lacks an object, a dynamic condition for anxiety. The emotional situation any writer must face is that anxiety and desire go hand in hand and obstacles, whether in the form of absence or lack, are not only inevitable. Losing the object is the material for both decomposition and composition.

In what follows I ask why reading for anxiety matters in understanding what happens affectively while trying to write. This will take us into more discussion on manifest and latent anxiety through examples of writers who articulate and disperse disquieting imagination as they write. From there we trace a third path with the idea that one can write one's way into and out of anxiety, provided that one links the dynamics of writing to a constellation of libidinal conflicts that emerge from matters of loyalty, affiliation, ideality, and finding one's own way.

Anxiety

"Then and now," Lyndsey Stonebridge observes in her affecting study of writing in mid-century wartime British culture, "anxiety fills the gap between reason and imagination" (2007, 2). Her question is psychoanalytical: how do we respond in writing to a history we fail to comprehend? Her method is to read into the work of journalists, novelists, poets, and psychoanalysts as presenting, "a kind of historiography of trauma" that provokes the imagination needed for thinking the afterwardness of "war time madness" (5, 2). Her study proposes what is extraordinary in deferred time. Writing resembles a state of emergency: a crisis for the writer and the emergent response to an event. The desire to symbolize what is out of order, however, affects the writing. At times, the writing will oscillate between exorbitance and depression. Anxiety, Stonebridge points out, "is what we feel when we are caught in a situation" beyond our thinking and our knowledge of it (2). And this catch is where the writer loses and finds herself. Affiliation with anxiety is a part of the danger being written.

Freud's essay written during the first war, "Thoughts for the Times on War and Death," begins with the incomprehensible: civilian disillusionment of commonality and "an altered attitude toward death" (1915, 275). To make sense of the senselessness of death in war and the breakdown of care and social response, Freud turns to writing: "We should seek in the world of fiction, in literature and in the theatre compensation for what has been lost in life [...] in the realm of fiction we find the plurality of lives which we need" (291). Except that this is the plurality that is being destroyed, and Freud argues further that we cannot remember our own murderous hatred, that war between aggression and libidinality. It is a grave speculation, but does bring

Freud to think more about how pervasive violence destroys the love of our emotional world, so tied to the love of the fragility and plurality of people. Writing and reading, Freud seems to suggest, reminds us of why we need anxiety, missing in times of war and only later returning as war neurosis. In mentioning what writers do, Freud is grasping for a depressive position, a means to sublimate into words the violence of the drives. Stonebridge (2007) as well presents this paradoxical situation. The writer, she insists, feels anxiety, and her case in point is a new reading of writing done during and just after the war that does convey trauma's volatility and sometimes fails from it. Anxiety *writ large* in times of humanly induced destruction forces the writer to account for the desire to write.

It is a difficult transition to move from representing war and death to picturing the benign and not-so-benign university classroom, although we can observe that education receives what the social cannot repair, that learning repeats its breakdowns without knowing why, and that before students and teachers are able to prepare, they are unwitting witnesses to the human condition through their crisis with education.

In everyday classroom scenes the little traumas, or narcissistic blows, felt as persecutory, affect the writer. Winnicott insists that ordinary learning carries on something extraordinary: "The anti-social tendency," Winnicott notes "appears in the normal or near normal child, where it is related to the difficulties that are inherent in emotional development" and "is characterized by an *element in it which compels the environment to be important*" ([1956] 1994, 120, 123; italics original). When Winnicott writes of the anti-social tendency, he is referencing the vicissitudes of ordinary frustration and aggression and the need for a witness. The anti-social tendency on this view is not a diagnosis but a mechanism for hope that the response to frustration will be of a different order than the provocation that the outburst brings, and that the environment, meaning the responses of others, will be able to stand the revolt without taking revenge. To press this point further, if one is to write what is on one's mind, an anti-social tendency is needed. We are moving into an area of the psychical experience of writing and, as we shall see, the intermingling of phantasy and reality with love and hate are major turning points in the untold story of the writing block.

Symptoms

Freud's great statement on anxiety, "Inhibitions, Symptoms and Anxiety," arrives late in the development of his theory; and it is where he changes his mind (1926). His first topology of libido posited that repression of intolerable ideas causes anxiety. In his second structural theory, populated by the agencies of id, ego, and super-ego, the sequence is reversed: anxiety instructs the ego's many defenses against danger and helplessness. In centering anxiety as both a signal of danger (automatic) and a question of from where the danger comes (phantasmic), Freud's theory of neurosis intertwines the catastrophe of the ego losing love with the problem of the loss of imagination. And there is a problem in communicating. Thirty seven pages into his tome on anxiety he admits the confusion: "It is almost humiliating that, after working so long, we should still be having difficulty in understanding the most fundamental facts […] If we cannot see things clearly we will at least see clearly what the obscurities are" (1926, 124). The obscurity belongs to the ego's mechanisms of defense.

Freud's second addenda of the inhibition paper clears a new path: "Anxiety [*Angst*] has an unmistakable relation to *expectation*: it is about [before] something. It has a quality of *indefiniteness and lack of* object" (165; italics original). We return to this problem later, though for now can note that in writing, the lack of an object presents as a blank page, missing ideas, loss of words, and the abstention of the self or other only brings sad conviction to the writer's despair. The so-called writing block appears as a terrible punctuation mark for this entire nothing. All of this is quite obscure, as if it happens without a subject.

Freud's essay on inhibitions contains a discourse on the ego's many means of defense against anxiety. Of interest to my discussion are two of them: undoing what has been done and isolation

(1926, 119). As for these defenses, we can note that in the situation of a writing block or the writing inhibition, undoing the writing — either through endless editing, harsh comments that seem to kill off an idea before its time, and never letting go — are key obsessional activities. Isolation of affect further disrupts by denying the meaning of the block as a piece of emotional life, keeping the writing to oneself, thinking one citation will wreck another so conflicting ideas are kept separate or even forgotten, and feeling persecuted should thoughts have to be put together. A conflict is being written. The anxiety that joins these defenses, it seems to me, concerns the worry that having one's say can only mean being sent into exile as punishment for one's ideal. Here, the dejected writer believes she will never be published, that there is no place for her work, and that no one cares. It is a paradox that the defense of isolation — keeping things from touching — brings closer the problem of associations that constitute psychical reality. Freud understands the dilemma this way: "The experience is not forgotten, but instead it is deprived of affect, and associative connections are suppressed or interrupted so that it remains as though isolated and is not reproduced in the ordinary process of thought" (1926, 120). Touching involves putting ideas together, needed for thought and for erotic activities. It seems that the defense of isolation plays out a prohibition against touching words and being touched by words.

The Letter

We can observe the painfulness of admitting these defenses and working through them in a letter Winnicott wrote to Melanie Klein on November 17, 1952 (Rodman, 1999). Klein had invited Winnicott to write a chapter for a book she was editing and the letter he wrote explained why he could not write for her. It had to do with his conviction that Klein only wanted compliance to her theories and that he wished to develop his own views as separate from hers. We can see the anti-social tendency as a needed position but also a hope that the other will respond without further persecutory anxiety. His letter is excruciating to read: he admits a failed analysis with his past analyst Joan Riviere, one of the editors of the book to which he refuses to contribute; he is writing to Klein, who supervised some of his analytic training; and, he is launching a stringent critique on Klein's views, including his wish to destroy them. It is a letter that declares the personal cost of his freedom of thought:

> I am writing this down to show why it is that I have a real difficulty in writing a chapter for your book although I want to do so so very badly. This matter which I am discussing touches the very root of my own personal difficulty so that what you see can always be dismissed as Winnicott's illness, but if you dismiss it in this way you may miss something which is in the end a positive contribution. My illness is something which I can deal with in my own way and it is not far away from being the inherent difficulty in regard to human contact with external reality. (Rodman 1999, 37)

We do not have Klein's response and only occasionally, through footnotes, did Klein mention Winnicott's work. Winnicott, however, will continue to write on the problems Kleinian formulations repeat; he will admit his hostility through the concept of the anti-social tendency and in his 1947 argument, "Hate in the Counter-Transference," he will reverse Klein's formulation of the baby's hatred of the mother (1992). It is the mother who must hate the baby and must know this hatred so well that she can surrender to love. So it is with the writer and her dependency on words. The writer must hate the writing and know this so well that she can surrender to the writing baby.

The psychoanalyst Ronald Britton discussed Winnicott's letter in his paper on publication anxiety (1994). Britton was addressing the analyst's anxiety in publishing her or his work: worries about putting forth a declining or unpopular theory, of not being original enough, of being disloyal to one's analyst, and of having to face a matrix of hostility that divides psychoanalytic societies into warring factions. He points out that anxiety also musters an intense epistemophilic drive to communicate to the other what one knows, along with an accompanying fear that either no one will care or the writer will be condemned as wrong or crazy. The defenses involve a great deal of splitting into good and bad, undoing what has already happened, and isolation. This "no one" may present as a real someone, such as the angry teacher, the stingy academic apparatus, the disappointed mother, and yet, as figurations of agony, "no one" is in the writer's mind and may include phantasies of the indifferent audience, the hostile ones who read only to attack ideas, the disappointed ones who cannot be moved, and those the writer may put to sleep. It is important to remember that these bellicose characters wager with the writer's mind, and Winnicott's letter admitted such poignancy when he wrote of his own illness as the "inherent difficulty in regard to human contact with external reality" (Rodman 1999, 37). The fear may well be real angst, as Winnicott's letter shows. And while sadism at its height in both academic and psychoanalytic culture seems to justify the persecutory thoughts and fears of retaliation, phantasies themselves are the anxiety and the defense against them. Common defenses carry conviction that the writer is smarter than anyone can ever understand, that the writer wishes to destroy the other's ideas, that the influence of others is a sign of weakness, and that the writer must go it alone. Britton raises Harold Bloom's (1973) idea of the anxiety of influence and, leaning on the early Oedipal situation as discussed by Klein, Britton goes on to argue that the writer is caught in conflicting wishes to create something novel, to join with others, to become one's own origin, and to exceed what has already been done.

There are, for Britton, two external and psychical pressures that tear at desire: "One is fear of rejection by the primary intended audience, and the other is fear of recrimination by colleagues with whom the author is affiliated and possible exile from them" (1994, 1213). Both involve the anticipation of isolation and the loss of love. I have already mentioned Klein's view that parting and loneliness go hand in hand, and I understand Britton to be suggesting that the defenses against anxiety in the form of undoing and isolation are, paradoxically, the first places of writing. Britton's contribution turns to the writer's phantasies, and he can then describe what happens if the anxiety goes unrecognized by the writer: "If it is denied it may result in a superficial, complacent text" (1213).

The writer's feelings of compliance, itself a conflict of loyalty, do turn into a "complacent text." The odd part is that one will have written anxiety into the paper by way of academic citations that don't belong, by backtracking on one's argument and slipping in the argument disclaimed, and by offering false homage to one's theoretical parents with stingy reference. Sometimes the enemy is made small through a footnote. It is as if the anti-social tendency so needed to write suddenly turns against the self. Britton came to these conclusions after analyzing one of his own papers. It is a turn to the writer as subject. "Sometimes," Britton observes, "it simply corrupts the language; at other times, the meaning of the discourse. I think anxiety about affiliation may be prevalent in psychoanalysis now [...]. There seems to be uncertainty as to whether psychoanalytic theory is in a state of fragmentation or integration" (1222).

To Write, Or Not?

By the time one arrives at the university, an unconscious history of having to write includes impressions of hostility; compliance, aggression, and revolt are ready at hand. Yes, the symptoms are fast and furious, as are defenses against them. And in the university, the pressure to write classroom assignments and dissertations, and then articles and books for tenure, along with the wish to put all this pressure behind, are abiding dilemmas made exorbitant in phantasy. Many of us are unable to survive what feels like a terrible loneliness agonized by rules that cannot be followed. But one of the more puzzling thoughts is whether one comes to the university to experience a writing block. It is hard to imagine, unless one considers that one arrives with a great deal of desire for belonging, affiliation, and having a say, along with doubts over whether such conflictive desires can be sustained or are even what we name as "realistic," a signifier of frustration and failure. Here, and drawing from my previous work, I wish to further develop the claim that what we call the writing block is a constellation of rents in emotional life and, to appreciate the psychical disparities, we can construct the sequence of phantasy (Britzman 2006; 2015).

When someone tries to discuss a writing block and the accompanying assignment that is either self ascribed or demanded by a waiting teacher, employer, or press, one first hears consternation as to why a writing block happens. There are too many words or not enough words. When someone tries to discuss what if feels like to have something hanging over one's head, or feeling that things are out of reach, or gets under one's skin, he or she may be referencing forgotten childhood complaints, but now with the acrobatics of self-disappointment at wasting precious time. We have heard such warnings before. There follows harsh judgments on the lazy self, a fortress of doubt as to whether he or she can really write at all. One is stuck. The disappointed writer may conclude he or she is best at fooling others and besides, writing is only pretense. Originality and the wish to write something novel seem to bring more danger, and then anxieties over copying what others have already said follow suit. The writing block takes cover in passive voice: it makes the subject go missing. And nothing can change.

Yet oddly, the writing block is filled with a crowd of bossy thoughts that are often written down, but these thoughts enjoin the would-be author to clean her house, delete emails, go for a run, shop, check emails, go on Facebook, pick lint off the carpet, get a coffee, search for misplaced objects, and imagine all other sundry imperatives. Evasion and evacuation render words as things. But the writer is missing. Literature, philosophy, and psychoanalysis weigh in on these matters with more writing.

Instead of a frenzy of activity, just the opposite occurs, as it did with Melville's enigmatic character employed in the dead letter department, "Bartleby the Scrivener" — whose only refrain when asked to do anything was, "I prefer not to" ([1893] 1997). In the passive defense, one may languish and hardly move. As the story's narrator complains, "Nothing so aggravates an earnest person as a passive resistance... Poor fellow! thought I, he means no mischief; it is plain he intends no insolence; his aspect sufficiently evinces that his eccentricities are involuntary" (28). It is true that no one would elect to possess a writing block; but "no one" is another term for projective identification, and it seems the writing block possesses the would-be writer.

Marion Milner's self study, *On Not Being Able to Paint* (1950) brings us to the heart of the matter. Published at a time when the question of creativity for ordinary people was just entering psychoanalysis, Milner's own disappointment with her painting—what she saw as "copies of appearance"—led her to question what the desire for mastery denies, and so she had to considered her mood (4). She was in search of the practical problems: what she took for granted, refused to see, and felt as absence.

> The more I thought about the direction in which this study was leading the more one thing seemed likely: that the original work in painting, if it was ever to get beyond the stage of happy flukes, would demand facing certain facts about oneself as a separate being, facts that could often perhaps be successfully by-passed in ordinary living. Thus it seemed that it was possible, in spite of having lived a life of independent work and travel and earning a living, to have evaded facing certain facts about the human situation, or only given a superficial acquiescence to them. Otherwise why was it so difficult to feel about, as well as think about, the separateness or togetherness of objects? (13)

The emotional facts Milner must face, face us all: the human condition absorbs what the self disclaims. Our vulnerabilities made from helplessness and dependency are evaded by anxiety, defenses, aggressions, and phantasies that have something to do with how we bear separation and union. The writer has to take things apart before they can be put back together.

"Children-no-longer"

To write without knowing one is blocked and have that be the paper written is also the dilemma that brought the psychoanalyst Paula Heimann (1899–1982) to create her term "children-no-longer." She was, for a time, a close friend, co-author, and analysand of Melanie Klein. By 1945 Heimann broke with Klein and turned toward the influence of the environment as the basis for the self's capacity for freedom. In the writing that came after, Heimann's focus was with the question of freedom in psychoanalytic work: the freedom of the analysand to find herself/himself, the analyst's capacity to move from the depressive position of repairing objects to the creation of new psychoanalytic experiences and techniques, and the analyst's freedom to relax and become a partner in the analytic adventure. Heimann's re-orientation is first hinted in the conclusion of her early paper on sublimation:

> As I have said, the inner world is a never-ending drama of life and action. Life is bound up with the dynamic process set up by aggression, guilt, anxiety, and grief about internal objects, and by the impulses of love and restoration; love and hate are urging the subject to strive for sublimation. The internal freedom to which I refer is a relative, not an absolute fact; it does not abolish conflicts, but it enables the subject to enlarge and unfold his ego in his sublimations. ([1939/42] 1989, 43)

Let me break my train of associations for a moment and quickly review some of my paper's main considerations that I see revolve around Ronell's (2003) insight that the writer is caught between freedom and unfreedom: freedom in the sense of possibilities yet to be known, and unfreedom in the sense of the anticipation of constraints that feel as if there is no way out. In summary, writing is an emotional situation where the words are between the poles of presence and absence. For Britton, one consequence of feeling caught between freedom and unfreedom takes the shape of publication anxiety (1994). Winnicott's view of the anti-social tendency is a provision for expressing frustration, provided that the environment can stand it ([1956] 1994). Barthes's solution for the writer — "the neurotic stratagem" — suggests that all writing (and teaching) locate the emergence of phantasy (2011, 269). Stonebridge (2007) places anxiety in the gap between reason and imagination, and with Klein ([1946] 1975) we grasp that anxiety is a situation of losing one's beloved objects and fear that they have been destroyed. With Milner's view, we take one more step, linking anxiety to disquieting imagination (1950). The creator must face both good and bad in the emotional world and create again, this time with feeling.

For Heimann, in her last paper, the omnipotent phantasy to disillusion is that of ideal beginnings. And she uses ideality to locate the tensions made while trying to write her way into her new concept "children-no-longer." There she expresses the passing of time and the remnants carried forward that bring her to articulate the difference between children and adults, freedom and unfreedom, continuity and dissonance. Of special interest is why Heimann spoke of her writing block as an unconscious phantasy that she saw being repeated throughout her paper. She speculates on why the latent anxiety contained in the phrasing "children-no-longer" was so difficult to release.

Heimann was eighty years old when she wrote "Children and Children-No-Longer" ([1979/80] 1989). She was asked by J.-B. Pontalis to contribute a paper about her work and focus on her responses to being with a child. She must have felt she was assigned a school essay and the order to write. Her first three sentences play in the field of the anti-social tendency:

> I start with the first ideas that came into my mind immediately after reading J-B. Pontalis's invitation to take part in a project that I warmly welcome. The word "ideas" is not quite correct. What occurred to me were pictures, scenes, memories of contact with children outside my professional activities. (324)

It takes Heimann quite a while to turn to the clinic. Before that, she provides lovely anecdotes of very young children's emotional logic that often seem improbable to the harried adult who has forgotten her or his childhood. Perhaps she is discussing her transference affairs with Pontalis. She returns to the "warm welcome" of being asked to write the paper in a short section titled "Editorial Demands and Strictures." There, hostility is given air.

> So far, I realize, I have reacted only to J-B. Pontalis's personal letter, and that was easy, child's play so to say. Indeed, without becoming aware of it at the time, I behaved like a child, and by playing showed what I do, in fact, consider characteristic for children: they respond immediately and easily to a benevolent invitation to express their thoughts, to be active and creative [...] As I now study the demands and structures issued by J-B. Pontalis, the editor, things at once become different. I encounter difficulties with which I am only too familiar. An empty page stares at me, and my mind goes blank. (334)

The personal letter has turned into the harsh editor and Heimann's mind goes blank. There is no other way to present what has happened, except she continued writing and asked herself a question when she noticed her anger and began to "vent criticisms" (335). "Is it significant that they [the ideas] are hostile? I answer in the affirmative" (335). She goes on to write, "Perhaps I have again identified with a child, this time, when confronted with a stranger, not knowing how to start a dialogue, or with parents who for reasons of their own were unable to initiate contact, or respond gladly to the child's attempts at reaching them" (335).

The rest of her paper plays in the land of hostility: she discusses ideas she hates, errors she regrets, and concludes with her disagreement on the order for the analyst to be neutral and uninvolved. There is, of course, an accrual of events that retroactively become the catches of recounting a life history and brought Heimann to become again the child she once hoped she was but is now no longer. Phantasy is written out, and its offer of "unlearning" is used to refine the pleasure in presenting her evolving views. We should note that the hostility or aggression she musters is the raw material for an affecting sequence: the writer's affiliation to a phantasy of origin, then the suspicion as to who is originating what, then an anxiety of being bossed, then blankness, and then to an idea she can properly destroy. There is an admission of aggression and a communication on the currency of writer's affects. Barthes's rule, however, comes after: "The principle is a general one: the subject is not to be repressed — whatever the risks of subjectivity" (2011, 3).

We have in a nutshell the sequence of phantasy and its relation to writing anxiety disclaimed, undone, isolated, and then rendered significant for working through. It turns out that the untold story of the writing block is unconscious, a constellation of conflicting phantasies of affiliation, loyalty, aggression, free association, and desire. We have been there before but without knowing why. Still, we must introject and project our discontentment — that "compulsion to symbolize" — to even begin to write over an index of loss. After all, writing reminds us of things no longer, and the return to words involves the estranging work of attaching existence to non-existence. Perhaps that open secret too was what Freud's (1914) ode to timelessness touched upon: *queer feelings, late, ordered, once again, school, strange, obey, and nothing happened.* In the game of *fort/da* a great deal happens under the sign of "nothing." It is after all the portal to the unconscious, to an affecting utopia that maddens the difficulties of communication and calls upon disquieting imagination. As for the writing assignment and our sense of the order to write, the anti-social tendency, however schizoid, will be our best resource, provided that we can overcome the prohibition on touching and being touched.

REFERENCES

Barthes, R. (2011). *The Preparation of the Novel*, trans. Kate Briggs. Text established, annotated, and introduced by Nathalie Léger. New York: Columbia University Press.

Bergler, E. (1947). "Further Contributions to the Psychoanalysis of Writers." *Psychoanalytic Review* 34: 499–68.

———. (1950). "Does 'Writer's Block' Exist?" *American Imago* 7: 43–54.

Bloom, H. (1973). *The Anxiety of Influence: A Theory of Poetry*. New York: Oxford University Press.

Britton, R. (1994). "Publication Anxiety: Conflict Between Communication and Affiliation." *International Journal of Psycho-Analysis* 75: 1213–24.

Britzman, D. (2006). *Novel Education: Psychoanalytic Studies of Learning and not Learning*. New York: Peter Lang.

———. (2015). *A Psychoanalyst in the Classroom: On the Human Condition of Education*. Albany: State University of New York Press.

Freud, S. (1914). "Some Reflections on a Schoolboy Psychology." SE 13: 241–44.

———. (1915). "Thoughts for the Times on War and Death." SE 4: 275–300.

———. (1926 [1925]). "Inhibitions, Symptoms and Anxiety." SE 20: 87–172.

Heimann, P. (1989). "A Contribution to the Problem of Sublimation (1939/1942)." In *About Children and Children no Longer: Collected Papers of Paula Heimann 1942–1980*, ed. Margret Tonnesmann, 26–45. London: Tavistock Routledge.

———. (1989). "About Children and Children-No-Longer (1979/80)." In *About Children and Children no Longer: Collected Papers of Paula Heimann 1942–1980*, ed. Margret Tonnesmann, 324–43. London: Tavistock Routledge.

Klein, M. (1975). "The Psychogenesis of Manic-Depressive States (1935)." In *Love, Guilt and Reparation and Other Works, 1921–1945*, 262–89 London: Hogarth Press.

———. (1975). "Notes on Some Schizoid Mechanisms. (1946)." In *Envy and Gratitude and Other Works, 1946–1963*, 1–24. London: Hogarth Press.

———. (1975). "Some Theoretical Conclusions regarding the Emotional Life of the Infant (1952)." In *Envy and Gratitude and Other Works, 1946–1963*, 61–93.

M' Uzan, M. (2013). *Death and Identity: Being and the Psychosexual Drama*, trans. Andrew Weiler. London: Karnac Books.

Melville, H. (1997). "Bartleby, the Scrivener: A Story of Wall Street (1893)." In *The Complete Shorter Fiction*, 18–51. New York: Alfred A. Knopf.

Milner, M. (1950). *On Not Being Able to Paint*. Madison, CT: International University Press

Rodman, R. F., ed. (1999). *The Spontaneous Gesture: Selected Letters of D. W. Winnicott*. London: Karnac Books.

Ronell, A. (2003). *Stupidity*. Urbana: University of Illinois Press.

Stonebridge, L. (2007). *The Writing of Anxiety: Imagining Wartime in Mid-Century British Culture*. New York: Palgrave Macmillan.

Winnicott, D.W. (1992). "Hate in the Counter-Transference (1947)." In *Through Paediatrics to Psycho-analysis: Collected Papers*, 194–203. New York: Brunner/Mazel.

———. ([1956] 1994). "The Anti-Social Tendency." In *Deprivation and Delinquency*, ed. C. Winnicott et al., 120–31. London: Routledge.

3

Learning How to Be a Capitalist: From Neoliberal Pedagogy to the Mystery of Learning

Samuel A. Chambers

Are we all capitalists? To claim that we are does not require any presumptions about personal belief systems or commitments to particular theories of political economy. We might say that we are all capitalists because we all live in social formations bound up with, connected to, and structured by the logic of capitalism (Chambers 2014). We have no choice, then, but to be capitalists; our choice is only to be bad capitalists or good capitalists. Marx suggested this idea indirectly and (in)famously when he described individuals within a capitalist social formation as playing certain roles, as bearers or supports (*Träger*) for the larger structures that made the logic of capitalism possible (Marx 1977, 1628).[1] The fictional character of Omar Little probably made

1   I am careful to say that Marx "suggested" such a notion, since Marx himself claimed something quite different — namely, that we are all *either* capitalists *or* proletarians. Indeed, one of the central elements at stake in both neoliberal pedagogy and human capital theory is the question of whether the players in the capitalist game are really all the same, or whether capitalism is just

the point more persuasively with his frequent references to the game: "the game is out there, and it's either play or get played" (*The Wire* 1.8; see Kamola 2015, 66). But if the game is the game, if we have no choice but to play it, then how do we learn to play? How do we learn to be capitalists?

This essay explores the question of "how to be a capitalist" by considering the relationship between pedagogy and certain elements of neoliberal economic theory. My primary and most general contention is that the fundamental idea of "human capital," a term and concept central to neoliberal capitalism today, remains thoroughly imbricated with a pedagogics. Put bluntly and somewhat more definitely: at the core of this strand of neoliberalism (but I suspect, and I imply, in neoliberalism more broadly) lies a theory of education, a specific vision of teaching and learning — in short, a pedagogics. For just this reason, any meaningful or viable challenge to neoliberalism requires *a pedagogics of unlearning,* in the very simple sense that any challenge to neoliberalism depends upon a prior unlearning of the neoliberal theory of education. In order to accomplish this "unlearning" of neoliberalism's pedagogy, however, we must first *learn it.* By this I mean that one (of the many) preconditions for unlearning the neoliberal pedagogics is to actually trace, analyze, and understand it. This is the case because neoliberalism's pedagogy goes mostly unnoticed and unremarked upon. Neoliberalism and neoliberals do not advertise this pedagogy as such, and this allows it to operate tacitly, sometimes silently, and very often for these reasons all the more powerfully. My task here will be first to detach and *specify* human capital theory as a significant strand of neoliberal thought (by giving a succinct overview/genealogy of neoliberalism); then I plan to unpack its tacit pedagogics (by way of a reading of Gary Becker's work), and finally I will offer some hints or suggestions of alternatives

the sort of game that requires very different players, operating according to very different rules. To oversimplify: is capitalism more like checkers, where every piece moves the same until it "earns" the right to move differently, or like chess, where from the beginning certain pieces can make certain moves that others cannot?

to the neoliberal pedagogy — what I am tentatively calling the pedagogics of mystery (which I think may well be a pedagogics of unlearning).

Neoliberalism and the University—The Traditional Story

So-called neoliberalism has, of course, already been tightly linked up to, and bound together with, pedagogical concerns. There is nothing new about thinking the neoliberal logic of capital together with issues of teaching and learning, since ours is the age of the emerging "neoliberal university." I use this term as a broad, catch-all phrase that remains powerfully multivalent. It points not only to the potential (or in-progress) takeover of the university by neoliberal capitalism, but also (perhaps) to the university as a site of resistance to neoliberalism. Here I have already begun to retell the traditional story of neoliberalism and higher education, but the full rehearsal of that story proves tangential to my project here. I only allude to that well-known tale at this juncture so as to contextualize and index my own specific engagement with one particular strand of neoliberalism.

The relationship between neoliberalism and the university has typically been framed in terms of spaces or domains or logics — that is, the university is a specific site, operating according to a particular logic, while market-based, profit-driven capitalism is a distinct logic operating on its own well-defined terrain. Neoliberalism thus names a phenomenon of encroachment — or worse, invasion or colonization. Within this conception, neoliberalism is taken to be a form of late capitalism marked above all by the *expansion* of the logic of the market to all domains of life, including especially all public institutions (or at least as many as possible).[2] On this account, neoliberalism's market logic encroaches upon, runs up against, or utterly

2 The literature on neoliberalism is vast and ever-growing; mine is not an attempt to survey that literature. For some useful inroads, ones that have been particularly salient for, and are most germane to, my thinking, see the following: Harvey (1982, 2005, 2010); Foucault (2008). For one important investigation of the differences between ordoliberalisam and neoliberalism,

overtakes the space of the college or university, while it simultaneously attempts to remake the very logic of education. There is no shortage of examples of this phenomenon: every time the university is analogized to a business, every time administrators are re-conceived as managers (with faculty as employees, and most of all, students as "consumers"), every time decisions are dictated by "the bottom line" — in all these instances we catch a glimpse of "the neoliberal university." Within this narrative, the university is understood as a space to be colonized by market rationality, business-speak, and the fundamental principle of profit (but usually masked in the language of balanced budgets and/or growing endowments). This explanation accurately captures a great deal about both neoliberalism as a practical force in the world, and about the transformations in university life, curriculum, and education over at least the past thirty years. The general story given here nicely explains, for example, the rapid growth in administrative and staff positions, the dramatic decline in the percentage of tenured/tenure-track/permanent faculty positions, the public defunding of higher education, the skyrocketing costs of college and university education, the explosion of student debt, and the list could go on and on.

Now, there is nothing really inaccurate about this standard story, and no doubt it gives us one significant way to think the relation between neoliberal capitalism, on the one hand, and pedagogics, on the other. It remains important to explore the questions of what happens to pedagogy — what happens to the conditions of teaching and learning under the terms of the neoliberal transformation of the university. Most of us who teach in the "neoliberal university" already have a strong sense of the basic answer: the very conditions for teaching and learning are at best impoverished and at worst utterly undermined by the forces of neoliberalism.

Yet such questions remain tangential to the purpose of this essay. Instead of looking at what happens to pedagogy when

see the recent Critical Exchange in *Contemporary Political Theory* (Biebricher et al. 2013).

the forces of neoliberalism arrive on the scene of the university — instead of asking what neoliberalism does to an extant pedagogics — I want to analyze the type and nature of the pedagogy that neoliberalism harbors within itself, internal to its own force and functioning. The standard story of the neoliberal university contains a blind spot in that it fails to see that neoliberalism has its own vision of pedagogy even before it encounters pedagogical institutions. In order to do this — in order to analyze neoliberalism's own pedagogy — I need to be quite clear about what I mean by neoliberalism, about where exactly I want to look when I look for neoliberalism's pedagogy.

As everyone now knows, neoliberalism is a term of growing capaciousness; the rise in its use to name or criticize various dimensions of contemporary capitalism has been accompanied by a loss of specificity in its very meaning. Indeed, many defenders of liberal capitalism have suggested that the use of the term by critics of capitalism serves as a sign of lazy thinking — that is, if you see something you don't like, call it a phenomenon of "neoliberalism" so as to disparage it. Of course, thought from the other side, these folks who ridicule any use of the term neoliberalism are usually themselves defenders of many of its principles, even if they refuse to use the term.

Nonetheless, I agree with the critics that clarity is required when discussing neoliberalism, and this is not just because of the contemporary broad use of the term, but because of the varied and uneven history of neoliberal politico-economic thought, on the one hand, and neoliberal political rationality, on the other. Let me then make a few categorical distinctions among the various strands of neoliberalism:

1. **Ordoliberalism:** A particular historical development in the history of economic ideas (and one that has surely influenced both historical and contemporary practices, policies, and ideologies), centered in Germany in the middle of the 20th century and hinging on the notion that the market can be allowed to work properly and effectively on its own if not hindered by the state. But this is not just laissez faire classi-

cal liberalism, since as Foucault eloquently puts it, the essential ordoliberal idea is actually to invert classical liberalism: rather than having the state act as a certain limit on the free market, the ordoliberals "adopt the free market as organizing and regulating principle of the state." Instead of a market supervised by a state, we get "a state under the supervision of the market" (Foucault 2008, 116).

2. **Neoliberalism as the "Washington consensus"**: This label refers to the so-called consensus on monetary (including monetarism), domestic, and foreign policy. Where ordoliberalism is marked primarily as a politico-economic theory, this variant of neoliberalism is best understood as a political rationality expressed in public policy. David Harvey is doubtless the clearest voice in analyzing this strand of neoliberalism (cf. Brown 2006); he describes it primarily as a response to the crisis of capitalism of the 1970s, and he sees it as an alternative to the mid-20th-century variant of embedded capitalism (Harvey 2005). Neoliberalism *disembeds* capital from state structures and institutions, using low-inflation monetary policy, financialization, and outright coercion (through IMF and World Bank policies) of developing countries to follow a strict path of capitalist growth. For Harvey, the 1990s Washington consensus on these key neoliberal principles leads to the reconsolidation of class power and domination.

3. **Human Capital Theory (HCT)**: HCT names a very specific type of American liberal economic theory, of which Gary Becker is the central figure. At its core, the enormous edifice that is human capital theory (which has now been applied to countless domains of economic, social, and political life) rests on one major logical move or assumption. The theory of human capital starts out with all of the core tenets of modern microeconomic theory firmly in place. Modern micro theory is the "theory of the firm," the economic theory of how firms operate rationally in the context of classical economic markets, of how a firm maximizes profit (by maximizing revenue and minimizing costs) in the face of other firms doing exactly the same.

Human capital theory makes just one profound addition to microeconomics. It says, simply: *what if we treat the individual just like a firm?* What if we reprogram all of modern microeconomic theory through the individual as an autonomous economic agent that seeks to maximize return on investment? This is my account of human capital theory; Becker probably wouldn't quite put it this way, but I would say that is because, to Becker, the idea of treating the individual like the firm comes almost naturally. Close readers of Becker see that for him the rationality of the firm in microeconomic theory simply is rationality *tout court*.

There can be no doubt that in the contemporary conjuncture these three strands of neoliberalism are inextricably intertwined, that their theoretical logics and their political rationalities are deeply intermixed, and that three different sets of ideas/logics mutually inform and underwrite one another. For example, Becker's human capital theory was developed at the University of Chicago at the same time as Milton Friedman's monetarism emerged, the very monetarism that plays a central role in the Washington Consensus. And the central ordoliberal idea of remaking the state through the logic of the market is mirrored in Friedman's economic ideas and in the IMF's polices. Any rich, comprehensive account of "neoliberalism" as a global phenomena must consider the interconnections and mutually productive relationships between these three distinct strands of neoliberalism, and this requires investigating neoliberal phenomena at the multiple levels on which they operate. For example, we might understand the overall force of neoliberalism as depending upon, first, the Washington consensus setting and maintaining the terms for global capital exchange, including dictating certain approved and prohibited relations between global "capitals," while, second, ordoliberalism specifies the proper and improper actions of particular state governments, all while, finally, HCT accounts for and prescribes the actions of the "individuated individual" (Marx 1857). Hence a great deal of contemporary politics might be understood as various attempts to mobilize or actualize the very rationality that is presumed to govern these three levels of neoliberalism.[3]

Of course, any such analysis would itself depend upon specific, historical engagement with concrete phenomena. Rather than study how and why they intertwine, my project here depends, instead, on isolating one particular thread of neoliberalism. Hence I now want to leave Friedman, the World Bank, Harvey, and the ordoliberals behind. My focus will be much narrower, as I turn directly to the work of Gary Becker, and particularly to his very early and fundamental articulation of human capital theory. Becker's work may be better known, and has certainly been well popularized, in his "application" of human capital theory to so many domains (e.g., family life, legal punishment and prison, etc.), but to get at his pedagogy we need to look at the basic elements of human capital theory — to see how he carries off the primary logical jump of his theory, which again is to treat the individual like a firm.

Gary Becker's Radicalization of Microeconomic Theory

In turning to Becker's writings I focus mainly on his 1962 *Journal of Political Economy* article titled "Investment in Human Capital: A Theoretical Analysis."[4] And I preface my interpretation of this work by saying that I came to attain both a deep appreciation of the power of Becker's thought, and a better sense of its influence, all through *teaching* him. In Spring 2014 I taught an advanced undergraduate seminar on the very topic, "How to Be a Capitalist." I assumed most students would read a certain irony in the title, especially when they saw the large amounts of Marx and decent doses of anticapitalist authors on the syllabus. But I was wrong about that. Almost half of the students who enrolled were ardent pro-capitalists in search of a defense

---

3 Thanks to Alan Finlayson for helping me to expand the account of the interconnecting of the neoliberal threads.
4 Further references to Becker (1962) will appear simply with page numbers in parentheses.

of capitalism appropriate to this post-2008 world; a significant number noted on the first day their allegiances to Ayn Rand. Needless to say, this was a very interesting group to have in place when we dug into the texts of Smith, Ricardo, Marx and others. But what surprised me most about the class is that even after reading and apparently genuinely grasping Marx's analysis and critique of the logic of capital, when we reached the end of the term the figure who most shaped my students' grasp of capitalism today, the line of logic and analysis of capitalism that they kept returning to over and over in order to articulate their own understanding of capitalism, was that of Becker — in this original, mathematical economics journal article. At the end of the day, a large portion of my students saw politico-economic phenomena through the lens of Becker. In a sense, then, as they became his followers, Becker became my students' teacher. This is not to say that my students simply dismissed Marx's delineation of the logic of capital, but in the end they somehow found a way, at least in their own minds, to do what should be impossible — to *reconcile* Becker with Marx, to see Becker's project as a certain extension of and overturning of Marx, one that allowed them to say, "yes, Marx is right," while then going on to affirm Becker's human capital approach.

So what did Becker teach my students? And to come back to my own primary claims, what does his work teach us about teaching? As I suggested above, I believe that we witness the clearest crystallization of the neoliberal pedagogy in Becker's now-classic articulation of human capital theory. I would be willing to call Becker's early work essential reading today for the very reason that it contains an obvious — and plainly important to the broader neoliberal project — theory of education. And all of this holds, despite the fact that even in Becker the pedagogics remains very much tacit. What is most readily apparent in Becker is not the pedagogics itself, but rather the theory's absolutely undeniable *requirement of a pedagogics*. Put differently, Becker's theory of human capital only works — only makes sense — if teaching and learning function in a specific set of ways, according to particular constraints, and with a specified set of goals or ends. More generally, then, we can say that Becker's theory of human capital necessarily presupposes a very specific, very definite understanding of what it means to teach, to learn, to know. We have to explicate — to unfold so as to unravel — this neoliberal pedagogy. Alternative pedagogies, ones that challenge neoliberalism, can then be articulated in relation to, and against, neoliberal pedagogy.

I start my reading of Becker by emphasizing that even in its original form — that of a specialized economics journal article — his articulation of human capital theory operates through the language of common sense. In the opening paragraph Becker states what seem like truisms: some activities or choices we make have an impact on the present, and some "affect future well-being." Betraying class distinctions that he would always resolutely deny, Becker offers the examples of "dining" for the former and purchasing a sailboat for the latter (9). He then buries his thesis within a straightforward declaration of his topic: "[T]his paper is concerned with activities that influence future real income *through the embedding of resources in people*. This is called investing in human capital" (9, emphasis mine). In other words, rather than setting out to prove conceptually or theoretically that we can or should understand humans as objects in which we can "invest" (a contentious philosophical claim) or that we can take capital as a set of fixed, static, and timeless resources (a potentially radical historical and economic claim), Becker instead presupposes the veracity of both of these positions and purports to report, almost descriptively or empirically, on the nature, extent, and implications of such practices.

As I show immediately below, Becker's early analysis develops the logic of human capital through the abstract, microeconomic example of firm-based training. However, Becker also clarifies in his opening passages that the fundamental ideas of human capital theory were born out of the primarily empirical project of "estimat[ing] the money rate of return to college and high-school education" (9). This context is not ancillary; it matters a great deal. The ahistorical logic that Becker develops emerges out of the empirical investigation of a concrete historical case, one from which the analysis can never be severed. That is, the project of developing "human capital theory" emerges at a particular historical conjuncture: the late-20th-century transformation of public education in response to the changing nature of capitalism in its relation to the state. Becker's rethinking of microeconomics occurs at the same historical moment as we witness the gradual transformation of "the disciplinary carceral logic of the 19th century school into the contemporary mode of individuated governance" (Finlayson 2015). As part of this transformation, logic itself (what Becker would call general training), not specific content (special training), becomes the thing to be learned in school, and thus debates over schooling shift from arguments about curricular content to the form and structure of the school. As I now shift to exploration of Becker's logic, I want to keep in mind the context that links human capital theory to the broader question of pedagogy.

Becker's presentation of the original — and up to the present, still fundamental[5] — argument takes shape mainly in the form of non-complex algebraic economic equations, but the basic assumptions and core logic prove straightforward. As I suggested earlier, when Becker begins his work here he is operating directly on the terrain of the core principles of the microeconomic theory of the firm. Thus he starts with the grounding assumptions that the markets for both labor and goods are purely competitive and in full equilibrium. These assumptions dictate that wages will be, as Becker puts it in one of the euphemisms of micro theory, "given to the firm" (10). In other words, the firm itself (or its managers) has no strategic say in determining wage rates, since wages will be determined by the purely competitive market forces, which means in this case, as Becker's first equation specifies, that wages (w) are equal to the marginal product (MP) created by the worker. Notice here that the standard assump-

---

5 The journal article reappears almost verbatim in every edition, including the most recent 1993 third edition, of the book (Becker 1993).

tions of micro theory not only set wages at a market-determined level (MP) but also establish "economic profit" at zero.[6]

Human capital theory comes into existence when Becker, starting with the equation MP = W, factors in on-the-job training, and in doing so derives an entirely new set of equations. Becker's logic proves (again) so straightforward — it does nothing more than develop the basic micro assumptions — that it can be easy to miss the radical nature of the conclusions to which that logic takes Becker, and his readers (and this is especially so for readers less accustomed to following the contours of a logic through equations). To raise the topic of job training for a firm means to inject a temporal dimension into the firm's profit-maximizing rationality. This is the case because on-the-job training functions as a cost to firms: if a firm devotes some of a worker's hours to training, the firm will pay the same overall wages, but the worker's productivity will be less than the marginal product "given" by the market (thereby reducing the firm's revenue). Yet, from the firm's perspective — and especially for non-economist readers, one cannot overemphasize that micro theory is just another name for the rationality of the firm — it may make sense to reduce revenue in the present if doing so can proportionally raise revenue in the future.[7] And this would be precisely the result if the effect of on-the-job training is to make the worker more productive in the future (to an extent that more than offsets present costs). So it would seem that firms merely make calculations about the present costs and future benefits of training, and from those calculations arrive at decisions about

---

6 Micro theory textbooks will distinguish between "economic profit" and "accounting profit" and specify that to set economic profit at zero does not mean that firms lose money, since "accounting profit" will still be positive. Accounting profit is then, somewhat circularly, defined as the profit that firm owners would capture in the best "alternative investment" of their capital.

7 My synthesis of Becker's logic (and attendant summary of certain tenets of micro theory) leaves out entirely the question of the time-value of money, or discount rate. The fact that the present value of future income streams is less than its numerical value (due to inflation) is, of course, essential to microeconomic equations, but it does not change the fundamental logic of the argument for human capital theory.

whether, and how much, to provide on-the-job training. If there were nothing more to it than this, Becker would have merely added another level of complexity to the decision-making and accounting practices of firms, and perhaps offered a window into understanding why some firms provide training (because it pays to do so) and some do not (because it does not pay to do so). He would not have founded a new branch of economics, because, as we can see, nothing in any of the logic up to this point has to do with the choices made by, or rationality of, individual workers; from the perspective of the worker — at this stage in the logic — one does nothing more than choose a job based on wages, and that job may or may not include training.

Here, however, Becker turns the argument in the direction of a paradox. First, he introduces the distinction between general and specific training; the former is "useful" (i.e., increases productivity) in all firms, while the later is "useful" only in the specific firm in which one works/trains. This distinction "forces" Becker into questioning the basic rationality by which firms decide whether or not to provide training. I would formulate the issue as follows: general training raises a "problem" (my term, not Becker's) for firms, since such training makes it irrational for firms to cover the "cost" of training (in the form of reduced revenues due to lower productivity during periods of training). This "irrationality" emerges because of the way that the temporal lag between the firm's expenditure on training and the anticipated return combines with the distinct nature of general training. The problem is this: a "trained" worker might leave the firm and take his or her "training" along, all before the firm reaps the rewards for its "investment" in the worker. Even worse, because general training provides workers with "skills" (much more on this below), and given the requirements of pure competition (in which $w = MP$) a worker will immediately reap the benefit of increased skills in the form of increased wages. Therein lies the rub: firms cannot "capture" any of the returns produced by general training; this means, therefore, that there is no competitive advantage to be gained by a firm choosing to pay for the costs of training. (All firms would prefer to hire workers trained at other firms.)

Becker works out this logic, and takes it to its radical conclusion, in a crucial early section of his article. He opens it by asking: "Why, then, do rational firms in competitive labor markets provide training [...] that brings no returns" (13)? Of course, by the founding definitions of micro theory, firms never do anything irrational — Becker's "rational firms" is a pleonasm — and thus the answer that Becker provides (on behalf of the firm) should be obvious (even if, for readers less steeped in micro theory, it might also seem non-intuitive). Becker explains: "The answer is that firms would provide general training *only if they did not have to pay any of the costs.* Persons receiving general training *would be willing* to pay these costs since training raises their future earnings. Hence the cost [...] would be borne by trainees, and not by firms" (13, all emphasis mine, cf. Becker 1993 loc 1727).

Hence the "problem" of on-the-job training is solved by firms' refusing to pay for such training, and instead displacing the costs of training directly onto workers in the form of lower wages. Given that the analysis operates squarely within the terms and terrain of the logic of the firm, some might be tempted to say that a firm, seeing the dangers of paying for training themselves, instead *forces* workers to cover these costs in the form of lower wages. But notice that this is not at all the language that Becker uses. Indeed, it is only for the first time, at just this moment, that Becker's narrative brings in the choices and actions of the worker. Once Becker's equations prove that it is irrational for the firm to pay for training, he shifts the logic and rationality on to the worker, and (almost magically, it seems) it turns out that just the thing that the firm needs the worker to do is precisely that which the worker "would be willing" to do. The key idea of human capital theory both emerges here for the first time, and is always grounded in this crucial logical turn. Becker's working out of the rationality of general on-the-job training turns workers into tiny little firms: rather than the firm investing in the worker in the present in order to attain a payoff in the future, we now have workers *investing in themselves*. The worker "invests" (in herself) by paying the firm to train her; that is, by accepting lower wages. The problem for the firm is thereby solved once the worker is no longer selling his labor-power for whatever wage he can get, but is instead making rational, firm-like decisions about return on investment.[8]

Of course, the end result of pretending the worker can and will act like a capitalist, is that workers are paid even lower wages than they would be in standard microeconomic theory. Becker derives a new equation that expresses the equilibrium in general training: $W = MP - C$, where C equals the cost of training (13).[9] That cost is deducted from marginal product such that the worker is paid lower wages than she would have been paid were she not being "trained." A reader steeped in Marx's interpretation of capitalism might pause, or even stare in wonder at this turn in Becker's analysis. Marx understood the very logic of capital to be itself fundamentally dependent upon a unique and historically produced social formation, one that has divided the world into two distinct groups — those who own the means of production and those who, because they do not, and in order

---

8   It seems worth pointing out an obvious oddness, and at least superficial tension, in Becker's logic: when firms act rationally to maximize return on investment, they refuse to invest in training, yet when workers are transformed into firm-like entities who also are meant to act rationally, they gladly choose to invest in training. Becker himself never even sees how odd this all sounds; nevertheless, his logic contains a consistent answer. The difference between firms and individuals here is that individuals can count on reaping the return on investment in general skills, whereas firms cannot.

9   The ideal case of specific training, and the practical real-world assumption that most jobs include some mix of special and general training, complicates the equations, but it does not fundamentally alter the logic whereby the costs of training are covered by the worker, who is now treated as a little mini-firm (but without any capital of his/her own) and who makes rational decisions about return on investment (on him or herself, since the worker cannot "invest" in anything else). Becker concludes that after factoring in a mix of special and general training we see that "firms no longer pay all training costs nor do they collect all returns but they *share both* with employees" (20). There is something sickly sweet about Becker's vision of the firm "sharing" costs and revenues with workers.

to survive, have no other choice than to sell their labor-power as a commodity. Given these structural conditions, wages are determined, according to Marx, not by the productivity of the worker, but by the "cost" of labor-power as a circulating commodity—a cost determined by the resources necessary to sustain the worker as a laborer, i.e., the cost of food, shelter, and other basic necessities for the worker (given specific historical and cultural conditions). Marx thought it was very difficult, and in the long run perhaps impossible, to reduce wages below the level of the bare subsistence of the worker. Now, I say a student of Marx might pause here in reading Becker, since Becker has at this juncture developed an argument for how the firm might pay workers *even less.*

In following Becker's argument, one can never forget that the logical switch he makes, whereby the worker is now thinking and acting "like a firm" in working through cost/benefit and return on investment calculations, and the logic of the worker is substituted for the logic of the firm, does not change the basic structural conditions of capitalism, in which the worker has no liquid assets to "invest."[10] Indeed, the only assets the worker has are those provided by the firm in the form of wages, and Becker is proposing that it is rational for the firm to pay lower wages *precisely because the worker rationally chooses to invest in his own human capital.* What, exactly, does the worker "invest"? Becker never says it directly, but the answer is as obvious and commonsensical as the rest of his reasoning: the worker "invests" *by making a loan to the firm*—in the form of lost wages.[11]

10 After all, a worker who had "liquid assets" (the language of modern economic theory) could use them to gain access to or ownership of "the means of production" (Marx's language), and thereby choose to produce a revenue stream by means other than selling labor-power. In other words, a worker who truly had the choice to "invest," could (and rationally, very likely would) choose not to be a worker.

11 This means that what I might call the "temporal risk" (the risk that an event will occur that prevents our investment today from paying off in the future) is shifted from the firm onto the worker. Recall that the key issue for the firm was the worry that in the case of general training a firm would not be able to capture its return on investment (because the worker might leave).

This means that the so-called "investment" in human capital is really nothing more than a new form of indebtedness of the worker to the firm.

I spell all this out — and I confess, I do so in far more words than Becker uses to develop his own logic — because it proves so hard to overestimate the fundamental conceptual, philosophical, and political *shift*: beginning with the basic tenets of micro theory we arrive someplace else, someplace significantly different. The firm wants to maximize its profits, so it wants more productive workers; and trained workers are more productive workers. Yet the firm cannot afford to train its workers if doing so will not increase revenues, and since the benefits of training only take the shape of *future revenues*, the firm cannot guarantee its return on investment. From here, Becker's argument *reveals* something that he himself never really seems to see: the firm will make its workers pay for their own training so that it, *the firm*, can maximize *its profits*. Thought from the side of the logic of the firm, there is never any space for the notion of "human capital." The firm does not maximize the worker's so-called "return on investment"; rather, Becker inserts the idea of worker "return on investment" — the essential idea of human capital theory, that the worker can "invest in himself" — almost as a *deus ex machina* in order to justify or explain why and how a firm will wind up paying even lower wages than microeconomic theory would otherwise predict. In one way, of course, Becker sees all of this clearly, since he shows that the firm will refuse to cover the costs of training of its own workers.

Yet Becker also believes, truly and fiercely, in the deeper idea of human capital that he introduces here. Within the structure of his logic, the claim that the worker "would be willing" to pay for his own training is at best an odd rhetorical flair, and at worst

> [*cont.*] Under Becker's revised equations, that risk of losing one's investment now falls to the worker, who, according to my terms, has made a loan to the firm that the worker hopes will be paid back in the form of future wage increases. But nothing guarantees those "future returns" to a worker who has "self-invested," since the firm might fire him, or he might be forced to leave the job for myriad reasons.

patent nonsense or intentional ideology. Nothing in the basic micro theory that Becker starts with requires us to consider or care about what the worker would be willing to do. Nonetheless, reading from larger swathes of Becker's broader corpus — in which he has "applied" human capital theory to so many domains of life — one clearly perceives his genuine faith in the idea of human resources as capital resources that can be treated just like money, roads, factories, and warehouses full of tools. And the bulk of Becker's oeuvre consists of expanding this idea, of "spreading the gospel," as it were, of human capital theory — and thereby rethinking our very understanding of capitalism and capitalist societies based on the idea that the human being is a capital resource.

The more one reads Becker, the easier it becomes to internalize and naturalize his fundamental logic. At times, one must willfully interrupt Becker's narrative, break through the underground, driving rationality that he constantly mobilizes, in order to throw his very logic into relief, and particularly to see its wider implications. This is one of those moments when one needs to turn away from Becker in order to see what should otherwise be obvious — namely, that the choice between investing in college or elsewhere is never really just a choice. Only those who have capital have that sort of choice. And, as Thomas Piketty (2014) shows so powerfully, the *vast* majority of people do not have capital. It is at this point that certain critical yet also sympathetic readers of Becker might suggest that his text forces us to return to Marx in order to explain the basic fact that in this social formation some own the means of production and everyone else does not. Moreover, it is *this fact* — i.e., the fact that everyone else does not — that forces them to sell the curious commodity called "labor power" — the very commodity that, according to Marx, makes capitalism possible in the first place. This gesture to Marx makes lucid a crucial dimension of Becker's project: the power of the theory of human capital is that it tries to undo Marx's very distinction. That is, if we believe, as Becker does, that we can "invest" in ourselves, then everyone becomes an investor, and capitalism becomes a naturalized terrain of equality — instead of a historically produced terrain of inequality (Becker 1993: loc 3374).

Above all else, the tendency of Becker's logic to erase Marx's distinction and thereby to make all agents in capitalism equal — for all of us are most definitely capitalists, in Becker's world — can explain precisely the appeal of Becker to my students. While Marx's explanation of the logic of capital appealed to, in a certain sense even persuaded, my students, that explanation came tethered to an idea they found irksome, if not offensive — that is, that they could not possibly be truly equal because the structures of capitalism made such equality impossible. By transforming them all (and everyone else in the world) into capitalists, Becker renders my students equal again. This is not a concrete or practical equality; indeed, my students can see clearly that the world Becker describes and that HCT advocates is one of fairly radical inequality. But it is a politico-ethical equality, one that explains inequality as itself a result of free choices by autonomous agents (hence a liberal equality, of course). As a colleague put it to me, our students "would rather have inequality without class than class equality." In other words, they would prefer a practical and fundamental inequality that is embedded in and bound up with a discourse that offers them the value of "equality" and mobility (freedom) over any sort of discourse that seeks to identify real, structural inequality.

Skills, The Stuff of Human Capital

How, then, can Becker substantialize this radical, and not only economic and political, but also ontological shift? When we say that we invest in ourselves, what does this mean? When we treat human beings as themselves forms of "capital," what does this look like? It is easy enough to count up dollars and railroads and airplanes, but what do we "count" or measure or invest in when we invest in "human capital"? The constant yet always enigmatic answer is *skills*. Becker clarifies on the first page of his original article that the very idea of the "human capital" approach evolved out of a study designed to investigate "the money rate of return to college and high-school education," and that the initial findings there indicate that earnings were always positively related to the "level of skill" (9, 10). "Skills" translate into "return on investment," while at the same time education and training are understood to produce, advance, or augment this very entity called "skills." Skills are the pivot point for the entire framework of human capital theory.

In one sense, skills take the form of a commodity; they are the answer to the question, "what do you get when you pay for education, or pay for training?" But skills are a very problematic sort of commodity, as they fail some of the first tests for any commodity: they are not a distinct object, they are not clearly fungible, and they are not alienable. Skills only manifest themselves in the body and person of the human being, so they cannot be a commodity like any other. This explains why skills are always the ultimate answer to the fundamental question of *human* capital, since unlike other forms of capital, skills reside within and are in many ways indistinguishable from the human person. It is in this sense that *skills are human capital,* and human capital is nothing other than skills.[12] Becker brings this idea to the surface when he later explains the difference between a firm's investment in research and its investment in workers' skills — something of a slip for Becker, since the investment in skills is usually portrayed as an investment made *by* workers. Becker explains that a firm's investment in research and development cannot be monetized without the help of patents and other devices that allow the firm to "establish property rights in innovations." In contrast, Becker continues, "property rights in skills [...] are automatically vested" (17). The "skill" is both the thing that the worker invests in, and also the thing that the worker already has — already *is,* as it were — once that skill has been "developed" by training or education (cf. Becker 1993: loc. 418).

---

12 Doubtless, Becker frequently refers to things beyond skills, such as health and well-being, but the logic of his argument boils everything down to skills.

In a way, then, it matters less what a skill "is" than how it functions, and for Becker the empirical results here are clear: more "skilled" workers make more money, and those with more education and training make more money, so surely (the logic would go) the increased money is exactly a "return on investment." Again, skills are the lynchpin of this argument: the worker "invests" in skills, through education or training, and skills "pay off" in the form of higher earnings. Without "skills" we would merely have a redundant or circular argument, since if we remove skills from the logic we wind up with the notion that educated and trained workers receive higher wages. This is surely the case according to Becker's data, but he needs to establish more than a relationship between training/education and wage rates. Under the individualist and rationalist terms of micro theory Becker needs to show that there is *first a choice* to pay for education/training that is then *followed temporally* by a return on this investment in the form of higher wages. Skills make the argument for human capital go: if the worker *pays for skills* and *skills then produce returns,* then we have a full account of the idea of human capital and of the individual rationality of the worker as being of the same sort as the rationality of the firm. Everything is explained by the "investment choices" of individual workers — that is, their choices to, and of how to, invest *in themselves.*

And this brings us to the crux of the matter: according to the terms and framework of human capital theory, education must be that thing that creates, extends, improves, or augments *skills*. Even though, as I clarified above, a skill cannot be a commodity like any other, it must still at least be analogized with a commodity, since education must be the practice that produces this good. At this point the now-dominant idea of institutions of higher learning as institutions of skills-production comes into sharp and powerful focus. Human capital theory has to insist, despite little or no evidence to support this insistence, that education makes skills. I imagine this logic resonates powerfully with all of us who have worked in the context of the university over the past ten to twenty years, since during that period of time colleges and universities (especially their administrative "managers") have come more and more to translate Becker's insistence into their own *insistence*: we must be creating skills.

Those of us who have taken up the roles of instructor in the university have been repeatedly told that precisely our job as teachers is to produce in the body of our students something called "transferable skills." I have no doubt that my story is commonplace: when I taught in Wales it was mandatory on all module guides to have a three to five bullet-pointed list of these skills. More important than any of the texts, themes, ideas, or history to be covered in any course was this apparently "concrete" (perhaps even quantifiable) notion of the "skills" that the class would somehow produce in the body of the student. In those very bullet-point lists, we can see a certain "materialization" of skills and an implementation of the neoliberal logic of human capital theory. In the requirement that such a list of skills be produced for each and every single module taught, we witness a clear (and materially powerful) expression of the core idea of human capital theory. The job of the teacher is to facilitate the individual student's rational choice to "invest" in themselves, and the teacher can only do so if what the teacher provides are "skills" that the student may later use to reap a return on investment. They pay us for skills, which they then leverage to produce a future income stream.

This language is now so ubiquitous that I would only bore you by multiplying cases of it. Yet I ask you to indulge me with just one striking example, one that twists the logic of human capital theory to the breaking point, and along the way perhaps betrays the emptiness of that logic in the first place. Beating all the odds, in Summer 2014 the us Congress actually managed to pass a bipartisan piece of legislation (quickly signed into law by President Obama): an extension of a Clinton-era jobs retraining program that essentially gives federal money to states and cities for training programs, while also, in a classical neoliberal move, "reduc[ing] the bureaucracy of the previous law by eliminating overlapping and duplicative programs" (Joachim, 2014). Praising this important legislation for its capacity to help overcome a "skills gap" between employed and unemployed workers, Obama gave a speech that contained a fascinating turn of phrase. The program, Obama declared, has "helped millions of Americans *earn the skills* they need to find a job" (Joachim 2014). Lest there be any lingering doubt that education and training are "non-market" forces, Obama deftly chooses the word "earn" to describe the relationship between unemployed workers and the skills that government-funded programs will provide them. This is not, the subtext screams, a government handout, and it is not even free education; this is an investment opportunity for workers who will not just "gain" skills, but will "earn" them.[13]

The Pedagogy of "Human Capital"

But if skills are what we "learn" in education and job training, then what does this tell us about those practices/institutions themselves? What goes on (or what must go on) for Becker inside the black box that is "schooling"? How must he understand the material institutions and the concrete practices that for him carry out this fundamental function of "producing skills" for the labor force? And to be more specific, what is the role of the student, the teacher, the "class structure" and the "learning environment" within the larger context of the teaching/learning of

13 The fundamental ideas of human capital theory — that human beings are capital, that one can understand individual logic as "profit-maximizing" return on investment — appear so dominant that just about everyone (aside from actual Marxists) buys into them. Thomas Piketty's now massively popular work provides a powerful case in point: Piketty proves to be a harsh and incisive critic of much of the logic and conclusions of both neoliberalism in general, and Becker's human capital theory in particular. Yet, Piketty utterly refuses to question the founding assumptions of human capital theory, taking it as unproblematic that any resource, including human resources, can be treated as capital (Piketty 2014: 304, 313). (Here one also sees why there can be no ultimate rapprochement between Piketty and Marx, since their definitions of capital — as stuff for Piketty; as a social process for Marx — are utterly irreconcilable and lead to radical divergences in their overall understandings of capital and capitalism. Nonetheless, Piketty's attempt to understand the overall historical force of capital does resonate with Marx in ways that ought not be dismissed by Marxists.)

skills? There are at least two main lines of response to this broad set of questions. First, we can go a long way toward filling in a neoliberal pedagogy based solely on the fundamental structure of the theory of human capital and the absolutely essential role of "skills transmission" in that theory. That is, we answer the question of pedagogics by way of a *brute logical deduction* from the core tenets of human capital theory, and it is in this way that we can, in essence, deduce a rudimentary neoliberal pedagogy from within the terms of Becker's human capital theory. That theory entails a direct, functional answer to the question of pedagogy, and it comes in the form of a tautological definition: a school simply *is* whatever institution produces skills in the sense dictated by human capital theory. Nothing else matters about it.

Yet there is no need to stop with this broad framework, since we have a second area of response as provided by Becker himself, who has a number of important things to say about the nature of schools and schooling—even within the framework of his original article, and more so in his expansion of the project over the decades. Indeed, never one to shy away from the formulation of succinct definitions, Becker tells his readers exactly what a school is: "a school can be defined as an institution specializing in the production of training, as distinct from a firm that offers training in conjunction with the production of goods" (Becker 25).[14] Becker's analysis develops in such a way as to specify the meaning of "training" that a school provides, and this is nothing other (and basically nothing more) than the production of skills (25). Here, then, Becker explicitly specifies what his theory already tacitly required.

The argument then takes a crucial turn, as Becker indicates that while a school may be in some sense a distinct institution, it

---

14 Here again we see the subtle power of Becker's euphemistic language: just prior to providing this definition, Becker has proven, using the logic of micro theory, that it is irrational for a firm to "*offer* training" for free—a worker must pay for her own training. Thus, the firm "offers" training in the identical sense as the firm offers goods: training is available *for a cost*. The difference being that customers pay the cost for goods, whereas workers pay the cost for training.

is in no way unique, since the school and the firm are at all times "complementary" in their functions and, on occasion, even interchangeable. Becker reaches this logic by making another one of his profound and far-reaching assumptions: *he treats the student as nothing other than a would-be worker.* That is, Becker runs the exact same equations for the student who goes to high school or college as he had run for the worker who takes a job. The worker's cost of training in the form of reduced wages is not at all distinct, according to these equations, from the student's cost of education in going to school. The only difference is that the student's costs include foregone earnings, so that the student's wages while attending school are equal to an MP "that could have been received" (MP_0) — that is, if the student worked full time instead of going to school — minus both tuition and other direct costs, along with the foregone earnings. Hence the equation for the student is the same as for the worker: $W = MP_0 - C$ (26).

Becker completes the logic by drawing what should now appear to his readers an unsurprising conclusion: "a sharp distinction between schools and firms is not always necessary: for some purposes schools can be treated as a special kind of firm and students a special kind of trainee" (26). Yet one should not let the inertial force of the logic obscure the radical implications of the theory: in just a few simple paragraphs Becker has turned all students into workers. Attending school is fundamentally about nothing other than choosing (or not) to defer wages in a rational (or irrational) way. According to human capital theory, we are all, including college and secondary school students, always already workers. We are investors in (our own) human capital prior to any external consideration of the meaning or importance of education. Indeed, education simply cannot be considered for Becker outside the frame of improving the return on investment in human capital.

I want to emphasize that in calling schools a "special kind" of firm, and students a "special kind of trainee," Becker himself thoroughly troubles the now-standard neoliberal account of the university as a firm that "sells" the "education commodity" to that mongrel hybrid, customer-students. Becker is not so much analogizing the university to the firm (such that the university has to sell a product and make a profit, etc.) but rather *incorporating the logic of the university* into the overall framework of human capital theory. Extending Becker's remarks on the special nature of the university, we might say that from his perspective schools are not designed to *become full-fledged firms*; rather, the purpose of schools is to function in support roles for firms themselves. Firms train (i.e., provide/produce skills) only as a secondary element of their primary function (to sell goods for profit), while universities primarily and exclusively train (provide/produce skills).

Yet this account leads to some thorny, unanswered questions for Becker, and, by extension, also for contemporary neoliberals: if a school has training as its only output, then is training its product, or does it have no product? Is the school meant to "sell" training? If so, to whom does the school sell? The only answer to this last question would appear to require making students into customers — a move frequently demanded and presumed by today's neoliberal university reformers. Yet Becker himself only ever treats students *like workers,* not like customers. How can a student be both a trainee worker of "the firm" and also that same firm's customer? We see that the attempt to conceptualize the school rigidly *as the firm* requires students to occupy two incompatible roles. Ultimately, any strict correspondence between the school and the firm breaks down, because in Becker's basic account we can say that the school is not just "a special kind of firm," but rather a unique kind: if the school produces only training, then its "output" is consumable only by its own trainees. Narrowly speaking — that is, working rigorously within the terms of Becker's logic — *the school has no customers.*

The attempt to contain the school within the logic of the firm is followed through more comprehensively and consistently in Becker than in much of the generic neoliberal "reform" of the university that we see today, but just like those concrete transformations that we witness in the present world, Becker's theoretical account leads to gaps and impasses. We can see lucidly that Becker's human capital theory tries to capture and contain schooling within the logic of the firm, and that his theory, unlike traditional micro theory, fundamentally depends upon and requires a role for schools and for pedagogy. But the reconceptualization of schools and teaching within the terms of neoliberal human capital theory is nowhere near complete in Becker's original account. Moreover, despite the fact that many of the basic tenets of human capital theory are themselves the driving forces for today's neoliberal reformations of the university, those very changes to universities often deviate dramatically from Becker in their understanding of the relation between a firm and a university.[15]

The Mystery of Learning

Becker's attempt to incorporate "the school" into his overall theory of human capital requires that he also tacitly develop a pedagogics to underwrite the basic notion of human capital. Yet in working through Becker's logic, and in comparing it to some

---

15 We can now also see that in working through Becker's neoliberal pedagogy we simultaneously bring to light a distinct and politically important understanding of the relationship between neoliberalism and the university. In other words, to see the neoliberal theory of human capital as a theory of education is to significantly reformulate the relationship between the university and neoliberalism. The university cannot merely be taken as under threat from neoliberalism as a hostile outside force, since neoliberalism already contains (a vision of) the university inside it. My primary goal here has been to unpack and re-articulate this neoliberal pedagogy — to show how it functions and what it entails. This reconstruction of neoliberal pedagogy allows me to conclude (in my next section) by pointing to the required future agenda of challenging this pedagogy, and not so much developing alternatives to it (we know already that those abound) as *mobilizing* those alternative pedagogies as critiques of and challenges to neoliberalism. Worth noting in this context: the end of the title of Becker's major book on human capital is, "with special reference to education." But even this does not constitute an addition or an applied example, since there cannot be "human capital" without the prior conceptualization of the human being as a creature who can be understood as being/possessing capital in the form of skills and knowledge. In order to defend the very idea of human capital, Becker and his followers must think education in a particular (and peculiar) way.

commonplace contemporary neoliberal ideas about the school as producing the commodity of skills for student-customers, we see that there can be no simple and direct correspondence between firms and schools. Becker's analysis begins with the assumption that the school is a type of firm, but as that analysis is extended — both within Becker's terms, and contra Becker, in today's neoliberal university — it begins to break down in a variety of ways. The school or university can never be easily or fully contained — not within the basic structure of microeconomic theory, nor within Becker's formulation of human capital theory. Of course, many of us might say instinctively and forcefully: all of this is because it never makes much sense to think of schools like firms, or to think of teaching and learning like producing and selling a product. My main project here has been to establish the centrality of pedagogy to human capital theory, and then, in turn, to demonstrate that such a pedagogy is untenable because it depends on a logically contradictory account of "the school."

But this primary project must be linked to and augmented by another. If we (teachers) aren't producing and selling a product, then what are we doing? And how can we articulate what we are doing more than merely negatively? Of course this question admits of no easy answer, for there can be no formula to capture what goes on when teaching and learning occur. I close here with just one suggestion: I draw a clue for a distinct pedagogics from another political economy — this time that of Marx. Marx was many things in his life, but unlike many canonized figures in the history of political thought and philosophy, he was not a *professional* teacher; he did not hold, or aspire to hold, a university post. Yet Marx was a teacher nonetheless, and in certain of his writings we can witness his pedagogy — one that I think can serve as a model for, or spur to, our own efforts to revitalize the sort of pedagogics that can help sustain today's university. And to sustain the university today means to challenge and resist the neoliberal hegemony.

One can locate Marx's pedagogy in many of his less-polemical texts, including in *Capital,* since in that work Marx is not stridently defending a pre-determined position, but rather working through, and working out with his reader, a certain understanding of the way the world works. An even better example of Marx's *teaching*, however, comes in his effort to summarize, synthesize, and present for a popular audience the dense and complex arguments of *Capital*. I am referring to Marx's paper "Value, Price and Profit" (VPP), which is the written version of a talk Marx gave in June 1865 at the First International. Unpublished in either Marx's or Engels's lifetime, this short paper served two purposes: its putative aim was to offer a full critique of the so-called "theory of wages fund." This theory — commonly held at the time, most prominently by John Stuart Mill — centered on the idea that within a set time-period, the amount of money available to be paid as wages was strictly fixed, and thus an increase in the minimum wage would have harmful effects on workers themselves.[16] At the same time, Marx also took this opportunity to draw from, synthesize, and re-present some of the most fundamental arguments of *Capital, Vol. 1*, which Marx was writing at the time of these meetings. In trying to condense very long, consistently complex, and incredibly dense arguments from *Capital*, and to do so in a spoken talk to an audience filled with workers and other non-specialists in political economy, Marx took up the de facto role of teacher. And VPP can be read productively as containing not only the outlines of Marx's understanding of capital, but also stark traces of a vibrant pedagogy.

Marx teaches his students about value, wages, price, profits, and about capital in general, not by specifying empirical facts or laying down general laws. His primary aim is not to render political economy transparent, but rather — and even for nineteenth-century observers and participants, but much more so as we read him today — *to restore a sense of the mystery of capitalism*. William Roberts provides an outstanding clarification of Marx's use of *Geheimnisse*, a word that "names both what is hid-

---

16 See the Editors' introduction to the English translation of "Value, Price and Profit" (Marx 1910, 2). I set aside Marx's critique of this now fully-discredited theory.

den or secreted away and the very hiddenness of it, the mystery attending its absence to inspection" (Roberts 2017, 79). Hence Marx is consistently misread when he is taken as one who seeks a deeper essential truth beneath false appearance. Political economy's *Geheimnisse* are not just mistakes and they are not a part of so-called false consciousness; rather, "they constitute a form of *common sense or practical wisdom that is essential* for people living in modern society" (Roberts 2017, 79, emphasis added). Marx as teacher approaches his students not by assuming that he knows lucidly something of which they are only dimly aware, but which he will render clear (Marx is no stultifier). Instead, he attempts to bring about a certain sense of wonder or awe at the general mechanisms and effects of the system of capitalism. This *sense of mystery* emerges throughout Marx's mature writing on capital — the term can be tracked consistently across the multiple published volumes — but it has been frequently and radically misunderstood. Rather than taking Marx as operating by the logic of inversion in which he will unravel all mysteries, defetishize all fetishes, pierce all false surface appearance to locate inner truths, we do better to see that Marx wanted first and foremost to make his readers, his students, stand witness to the mysteries of capitalism. One could work through a long series of examples here, but let me focus narrowly on what I take to be the two most important.

First, for Marx, the very idea of equal exchange is nothing less than a mystery. It is astonishing to Marx that a system of exchange can develop such that *all commodities are rendered equal to one another,* as long as we get the proportions correct. That xA *equals* yB[17] is an absolute wonder; it ought to stupefy us. Marx shows that there is a social process at work that makes possible the equation (and the genuine equality) of things that are not equal, things that are not even both things — entities that in one sense ought not even be comparable. Long ago, and in

17 The algebraic formulation conveys the simple idea that some amount x of commodity A is equal to some other amount y of commodity B. *Capital* goes on at great length looking at all of the different ways that commodities can be rendered equal (exchanged) based on the proper proportions.

an utterly distinct context, Jacques Rancière rightly and aptly called this "an impossible equation" (Rancière 1989, 108). Marx sets out to show how capitalism makes the impossible equation very much real, but to do this he must first get his students to see capitalism as a process that operates precisely on the terrain of impossibilities. In order to *explain* the mystery, of course, we would need to turn to the thorny question of the labor theory of value. Here I have neither the interest nor the need to entangle myself in those debates, since my point is much simpler: regardless of Marx's response to the mystery, his approach to teaching us about capitalism depends first on recognizing capitalism's mysterious nature.

He makes this same move when it comes to offering his own unique, and most powerful, contribution to our understanding of capital, in the form of his theory of surplus value. Again, I am not concerned to work through the details of Marx's understanding of surplus value as built on the distinction between, on the one hand, the magical commodity of "labor-power" that the worker sells (for it is all he has) to the capitalist, and on the other, the labor time that the capitalist actually takes control over and uses to create more value in the commodity than the capitalist paid in the wages necessary to sustain the existence of the worker. The important pedagogical point comes much earlier, when Marx asks the simple, yet so very deep question: where does profit come from? Marx insists that classical political economy has never been able to answer this question precisely because the political economists have never really *asked it*. They never see the wonder, the mystery of profit. This means that the political economy of Marx's time (and just as likely the economics of our time) cannot explain a fundamental dimension of capitalism, an element essential to all other economic explanations. Put differently, the classical political economists — whose very project is to theorize capitalism — fail utterly to *understand the fundamental logic of capital*. They cannot explain profit.[18]

18 Modern economics easily dismisses Marx on this point by defining profit quite simply as "accounting profit," i.e revenues minus expenses. Profit is real, they suggest, because we see it on business ledgers and Excel spread-

Their failure comes because they do not see profit as Marx does, as a mystery. Profit cannot be explained by way of today's so-called "accounting profit"; it cannot be explained by gaming the system, and it cannot be explained by nominal price increases. This is why in VPP Marx repeatedly advances the formula (to be proved): "profit is made by selling a commodity at its value" (Marx 1910, 20, and ff.) A capitalist system must have an element of genuine, productive *growth* in it. Capital must somehow, almost magically, *increase*; it must augment itself and continually become more than it was. This is what Marx means by the self-valorization of value, and what he expresses in the reduced form of the general formula for capital: $M \to M'$. As Thomas Piketty puts it, in a brief moment whereby he, too, glimpses the mystery: "that capital yields rent is astonishing" (Piketty 2014, 423). Piketty, however, refuses to dwell on the mystery[19]; where-

> sheets; hence there is no mystery. More seriously, certain Marxists follow the modern economists here, taking "the going rate of return" (i.e., profit) as an unproblematic given, and using the equations of modern economics to try to relocate the exploitation of workers elsewhere (Wolff 1981, 103). Other close and careful readers of Marx assert that in his resolution to the mystery of profit Marx "relied on Ricardian propositions" that led him to an untenable return to an "*objective* view of value," tied to the idea that "human labor-power has" a special "property" — namely "the ability, so Marx argues, to bring forth more value than was itself absorbed in its own reproduction" (Carver 1998, 63, 80, 81). Given this failure on Marx's part, the best way to understand profit is as a "bubble"; self-expanding value is made real because people believe it to be real — until, of course, they don't (Carver 2015). From the perspective of the pedagogics I advance here, all of these alternative approaches to profit fail from the beginning to grasp the mysterious nature of profit. The trick, says Marx, is to figure out where "accounting profit" comes from in the first place, and Marx is at pains to show that the Ricardian labor theory of value (not to mention the versions advanced by the "vulgar economists"), which posits labor as the objective source of value, simply will not do (e.g., Marx 1977, 173, fn 33).
>
> 19 Piketty notes his astonishment, but then quickly moves on. What might happen if he, or his readers, should pause before going forward? What Piketty calls an "astonishing fact" may be something much more than a *fact*— it may be in need of further explanation. Indeed, that M becomes M' is itself the thing we need to understand, and because of this, we should not extrapolate from our own capitalist formation (set up in order to make it possible for M to become M') back across all time and history so as to assume that all

as Marx lingers there for dozens of pages in *Capital,* and then spends dozens more attempting to come to terms with capital's self-valorization process through his own understanding of surplus value.[20]

I retell just the briefest snippets from Marx's story in order myself to capture some sense of his own capacity for re-enchanting the world by rendering it mysterious (Bennett 2001). What would it mean for our pedagogy to revolve around this fundamental dimension, this primary effort to render the world alien, foreign, mysterious? What would it mean to build a pedagogy on the premise and goal of instilling in our students a deep sense of wonder, of making it possible to return them (and for us to return with them) to that state in which we see the world as mysterious? Here is a (rather Socratic) hypothesis worth testing and revising: we can only truly *learn* when we take ourselves to be in a state of not-knowing; hence, learning depends upon approaching the world as if learning about it, understanding it, is not the same thing as knowing things and facts about it. We have to follow Marx's lead when it comes to the equality of exchange or the growth of capital, by continually asking not just our students but more importantly ourselves, "how does that really work" and "why is that really possible, what makes it so?"

Marx's pedagogy in capital offers a stark divergence and illustrative contrast with Becker. Becker presupposes exactly that which he ought to explore/explain/learn about. Marx takes capi-

---

"stuff" and "skills" can be called capital. Capital is a relation and a process, dependent upon a set of practices, presupposing a larger social totality to make that process possible (see Harvey 1982; cf. Harvey 2014).

20 As I have made clear in the text above, my aim here is not to solve or even enter the debates over how to explain profit or how to interpret Marx on the questions of labor and value. I confine myself to the specific question of alternative pedagogies. In this context, however, it is worth noting the significant contribution that Robert Paul Wolff makes to the always unsettled and always ongoing debate over Marx and the so-called labor theory of value: Wolff rejects Marx's own answer to the question of where profit comes from and provides an alternative that depends, as Wolff says in his own words, on "treat[ing] the workers as if they were petty entrepreneurs" (Wolff 1981, 111). In other words, Wolff, an avowed Marxist, implicitly relies on the precepts of HCT in order to "save" Marx from himself.

talism as a mystery to follow, to explore, to continually engage with. And the mystery of capital offers one powerful example of an alternative pedagogy, precisely because so much of the world we live in is premised upon the fact that capital is not mysterious, but rather quite obvious. One of the messages the (capitalist) world conveys to us is that we don't need to learn about it because we already clearly understand it. Marx transforms the very question of how capital(ism) works into a riddle. In thinking through the manner in which Marx responds to that riddle (and consistently renders it more, not less, enigmatic) — one that the political economists of his day, and the economists of ours, take as utterly straightforward and unproblematic — we may find a clue, or even rough model, for how we ought to think about our own reading practices, our own teaching and learning practices.

This is the moment, however, when the link between Socrates and Marx must be severed. The pedagogy of Marx and Socrates are linked because both challenge us to question the normal or the conventional. For Socrates, this means revealing to his interlocutors that what they took for truth or knowledge (*epistēmē*) was really only the dominant opinion of the day (*doxa*) — a common sense that was more common (shared by everyone) than it was sensible. For Marx, this means putting himself and his readers to work in order to demonstrate how much *work* institutions, norms, and other texts are continually putting in to produce the "normal" — including rendering us as "normal" agents who can only see confirmation of that very perspective. Both thinkers render the world more mysterious, but not in the same way or toward the same ends. *Socrates spiritualizes the world; Marx temporalizes it.* To say that Socrates "spiritualizes" the world is to indicate the extent to which the mystery of the world is, for him, a universal fact about it, precisely because the realm of knowledge is itself transhistorical and unchanging — the *eidē* are hardly even of this world, but they certainly are not subject to it. Hence, on some readings of Plato, the mystery of the world is all there is to know about it; Socrates' wisdom is contained only in the knowledge of his own ignorance, itself a glimpse of insight into the unchanging yet unattainable nature of *ideas*.

Marx, in stark contrast, temporalizes the very world that he renders mysterious. That is to say, Marx's pedagogy makes the world more opaque to us, not so that we come to think of the world itself as external to us (a roughly "religious" view), out there and ultimately unknowable, nor so that we grasp the world as out there and waiting to be known properly only by the appropriate empirical techniques of measuring it (a roughly "scientific" view). Rather, Marx's mysterious world is more complicated than any of those other visions, since Marx's world is one that we ourselves are implicated in. His is a dynamic world in the making, and thus he shows us not radical unknowability but radical incompletion. Marx makes the world mysterious not because only scientists and priests can ever know it, but because we can only ever know it through our actions in it — actions that do much more than "add" to the world, but transform it completely.

I suggest we read Marx's remarks to workers at the First International in just this context. In his presentation of VPP, Marx explains to his audience that if you cannot explain profits by assuming that commodities sell at (not above or below) their values, then in that case, he continues: "you cannot explain it at all." Marx then notes the counterintuitive nature of this move, when he says that "this seems paradox and contrary to every-day observation"; however, he continues in a powerful pedagogical twist, "It is also paradox that the earth moves round the sun, and that water consists of two highly inflammable gases. *Scientific truth is always paradox*" (Marx 1910, 17, emphasis mine). This claim returns us to the double sense of *Geheimnisse*: it is not that we first have a mystery, and then we have its resolution in bare, simple truth. Rather, truth is itself mysterious. But we ourselves are part of the mystery.

Pushing toward broader implications for a pedagogics — and putting aside contentious debates over so-called "science" — let us leave the political economists behind so that we might turn our focus toward truth or knowledge, or better, toward teaching and learning. In order to do so I would translate these statements of Marx into the following pedagogical principles: to learn is to discover mystery; to know is to know paradox. And yet, these pedagogical principles ought not and cannot be statements of fact or articulations of knowledge/truth; they must be subjunctive proclamations that force an ontological shift by altering the very form of the verb "to be." Put differently, this means that to teach is always to proceed "as if," and thus our pedagogical principles must not be a series of commands or dictates, but rather a string of "what ifs." What if we approached teaching as if all learning were paradox? What if learning exceeded, or even had nothing to do with, the accumulation of facts and information? What if "skills" were nothing other than the pure fabrication and phantasmic hypostatization of neoliberal theory? What if a core element of the school or the university were uncontrollable, uncooptable by the logic of neoliberalism? What if we could *unlearn* the neoliberal pedagogy and recommit to these very pedagogic principles of the mystery of learning?

REFERENCES

Becker, G. (1992). "Investment in Human Capital: A Theoretical Analysis." *Journal of Political Economy* 70.5:9–49.

———. (1993). *Human Capital: A Theoretical and Empirical Analysis, with Special Reference to Education.* Chicago: University of Chicago Press.

Bennett, J. (2001). *The Enchantment of Modern Life: Attachments, Crossings, and Ethics.* Princeton: Princeton University Press.

Biebricher, T., Nicolas Jabko, Anita Chari, and Josef Hien. (2013). "Critical exchange on neoliberalism and Europe." *Contemporary Political Theory* 12.4: 338–75.

Brown, W. (2006). "American Nightmare: Neoliberalism, Neoconservatism, and De-democratization." *Political Theory* 34.6: 690–714.

Carver, T. (1998). *The Postmodern Marx.* Manchester: Manchester University Press.

———. (2015). Email to Author, 15 February.

Chambers, S. (2014). *Bearing Society in Mind: Theories and Politics of Social Formation.* London: Rowman & Littlefield International.

Foucault, M. (2008). *The Birth of Biopolitics: Lectures at the Collège de France, 1978–79.* New York: Palgrave Macmillan.

Harvey, D. (1982). *The Limits to Capital.* Chicago: University of Chicago Press.

———. (2005). *A Brief History of Neoliberalism.* Oxford and New York: Oxford University Press.

———. (2010). *The Enigma of Capital: And the Crises of Capitalism.* New York: Oxford University Press.

———. (2014). "Afterthoughts on Piketty's Capital." http://davidharvey.org/2014/05/afterthoughts-pikettys-capital/. (Accessed March 8, 2015).

Joachim, B.D.S. (2014, July 22). "Obama Signs New Job-Training Law." *The New York Times.*

Kamola, I. (2015). "The Politics of Knowledge Production: On Structure and the World of *The Wire*." In *The Politics of HBO's* The Wire: *Everything is Connected,* ed. Shirin Deylami and Jonathan Havercroft, 59–86. London: Routledge.

Marx, K. (1910). *Value, Price, and Profit.* Chicago, IL: C.H. Kerr & Company.

———. (1977). *Capital, Volume One.* New York: Penguin.

Piketty, T. (2014). *Capital in the Twenty-First Century.* Cambridge, MA: Harvard University Press.

Rancière, J. (1989). "The Concept of 'Critique' and the 'Critique of Political Economy' (From the Manuscripts of 1844 to Capital)." In *Ideology, Method, and Marx: Essays From Economy and Society,* ed. Ali Rattansi, 74–180. London and New York: Routledge.

Roberts, W. (2017). *Marx's Inferno: The Political Theory of Capital.* Princeton: Princeton University Press.

Wolff, R.P. (1981). "A Critique and Reinterpretation of Marx's Labor Theory of Value." *Philosophy & Public Affairs* 10.2: 89–120.

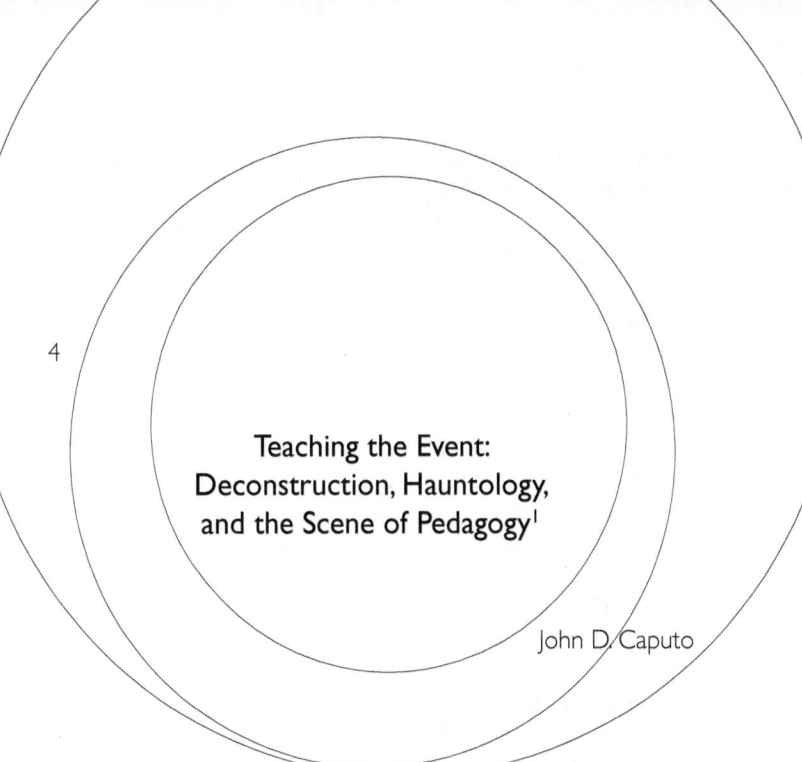

4

Teaching the Event: Deconstruction, Hauntology, and the Scene of Pedagogy[1]

John D. Caputo

Education is an event. More precisely, it is haunted by the event. All the aporias of education, all its desires and frustrations, everything we love about education and everything that drives us mad, has its ground without ground not in an ontology or a methodology or a psychology of education but a hauntology. Only as a hauntology is the philosophy of education possible. That will be my hypothesis today.[2]

Allow me to begin with a scene you will all find familiar. When our children were still attending the public schools in our township, I stood for election for the school board. We were try-

---

1 The current essay was delivered as the 2012 Kneller Lecture, Pittsburgh, March 24, 2012. A slightly altered version has also appeared in *Philosophy of Education* 2012, ed. Claudia W. Ruitenberg.
2 The leitmotif of "hauntology" used in this paper is taken from Jacques Derrida, *Specters of Marx: The State of the Debt, The Work of Mourning, and the New International,* trans. Peggy Kamuf (New York: Routledge, 1994), 10, et passim.

ing to elect the first Democrat in the history of the township school board, and my appointed task was to run to the left of the person we were really trying to elect and make her appear moderate. Needless to say I relished the task. My only hesitation was the fear that I would be collateral damage, that is, that we would succeed so well that I too would be elected and then I would have to attend all the school board meetings. In that case, my first official act would have been to demand a recount. The issue was, of course — what else? — school taxes. What would have been very funny about the campaign, were it not also so serious, was that we had only one real issue with which to appeal to our Republican friends — not the welfare of the children, not fairness to the teachers, not the wellbeing of the country, not the future. The only thing that appealed to them was property values. The local realtors made generous use of the well known quality of the township schools in advertising, which drove up property values, and if the voters wrecked the schools, they would destroy their own property values. You get what you pay for. They heard that argument, and we were able to elect our moderate candidate.

The other thing that struck me during the campaign was the threat that the teachers had put on the table to spook the township, that if these issues were not fairly resolved, they would "work the contract." As you well know, that means they would do everything agreed to in the contract but not a thing more, not a thing that the contract did not spell out — not a single extra moment after the dismissal bell, not a single extra phone call to a parent, not a single extra session with a student, not a single extra effort in any regard on any matter that could not be legally demanded of them. Just the contract. Of course, this was a specter, a nightmare, a monster; because everyone knows that it is precisely this something extra that makes the difference, that makes the schools run. The teachers must make the contract work. If they work the contract, the contract will not work.

The Aporias of the Gift

While this scene is a familiar one to you, allow me to defamiliarize it by redescribing it in the framework of "deconstruction" and the logic, or rather alogic, of the "gift" in a deconstructive analysis. My goal is to take a familiar scene found with unhappy regularity in almost any school district in America and to redescribe it as a scene overrun by the aporias of contemporary French philosophy. This may seem like an attempt to explain something perfectly clear by means of something very obscure, like explaining why the roof leaks by starting with quantum mechanics. If so, I apologize. Well, on second thought, I do not. That is why I am here.

This is, in my view, an exquisitely deconstructive scene, an almost perfect illustration of the dynamics of the "gift" in deconstruction.[3] The gift seems to be the simplest of things: A gives x to B. Nothing could be simpler. But notice how difficult, how elusive this is; it's almost impossible, we might say. Maybe even the impossible itself. All that A wants to do is to give x to B, and to do so generously, without the expectation of return, freely, gratuitously:

A: Take it, it's yours.
B: But you should not have done that.
A: Of course not, that's why it is a gift.
B: I don't know how to repay you.
A: I am not asking you to repay me. It's a gift. Take it, enjoy.
B: I will always be in your debt.
A: I don't want you to be in my debt. I want you to enjoy it.
B: You are too kind.
A: I am not trying to be kind. I just want you to have this gift.

---

3   See Jacques Derrida, *Given Time, I: Counterfeit Money,* trans. Peggy Kamuf (Chicago: University of Chicago Press, 1991), ch. 1 for a splendid presentation of this aporia.

I am trying to give a gift, to give something away, something that leaves my possession and thereafter leads another life I cannot control. Take the gift, it is yours. But as soon as the gift is given the gift begins to annul itself, to establish an economy in which the one to whom the gift is given incurs a debt, an obligation, which will impel him or her to find some way to repay this gift and discharge this debt, even while the more purely the giver tries to give this gift, the more generous the giver seems. So the result is that the one to whom something is given ends up in debt, while the giver who has given something away has come out ahead. As soon as it is given, the gift begins to be annulled. Derrida's advice is performative: in the face of this "aporia," he tells us to "give," all the while knowing and appreciating the traps that lie hidden in giving. Know how giving annuls itself, but nonetheless give, take the leap of faith in the gift and give, madly as it were, against all knowledge, in a moment of giving that tears up the circle of the economy.

That aporia is the main interest of Derrida's analysis of the gift, but there is a second aporia that his analysis also uncovers, which is of no less interest to us here. This time the accent in the aporia falls not on the side of the gift itself but on the side of the economy, which shows up in the second piece of advice Derrida gives us, complementary to the first, which is to "give economy a chance." This is a typically multivalent expression which means, first of all, do not simply dismiss the idea of an economy as the work of an evil demon, but "give it a break," as we would say in English. After all, the economy is what is all around us and, in a certain sense, it is really the only thing that exists, while the gift does not quite exist but tries to "insist" in the midst of what exists, where it is all but overwhelmed, nearly invisible, nearly nothing at all, like a ghost. But Derrida also means this in a much more literal sense, to let the element of "chance" gain admittance to the economy, to inject a chance into the veins of the economy, to let the economy be disturbed by the chance of the gift, or by the gift of chance, to admit the chance of what he calls the "event," the incoming of the event. So the "gift" is like an inexistent but insistent spirit, like a specter that haunts the wheels and pulleys and clanking gears of the economy.

The gift is not given in exchange for something else; it is not part of a calculated *quid pro quo*. It is not required or necessary, not demanded or commanded. But by the same token, if the gift is withheld, the economy contracts into a monster, and instead of providing the scene of the event, it will become a nightmare. If the economy is not breached by these moments that exceed the economy, the economy seizes up. If we remain absolutely within the law, the result will be the worst injustice and the law will be a monster. So not only is the pure gift impossible, but so also is a pure economy. Absent the gift, the school would be an impossible place to be. The innumerable, invisible, ghostly gifts the teachers make are all gratuitous, extra, in excess of the economy, yet they are all absolutely necessary. The gift must be given, yet it is not a gift if it is compelled, coerced, demanded. If you give me your help out of a sense of duty, it is not a gift, and I might just as soon do without it. We ought to give a gift where there is no question of an "ought" or of "owing." The gift is given without owing, without ought, without why. I hasten to add that this dynamic of the need for the gift does not merely apply one-sidedly to the teachers alone, that it applies across every sector of the system, from top to bottom. It applies no less to the top, to the administrative powers that run the school — I am not recommending a policy of exploiting the good will of teachers. Pedagogy without why does not mean teaching without pay and working for nothing. It applies no less to the students, who will not get by if all they want to do is get by. Here is the first hauntological situation: those of us who spend our lives in the school find ourselves situated *between* the gift and the economy. We lead haunted lives, charmed or haunted by a call which is too "weak" and spectral to be an imperative even as we must conduct the ordinary business as usual of the economy of the world.

The Event

It is the "event" that produces this spectral effect. Ghosts are neither entirely present, which is why we don't believe in them, nor entirely absent, which is why we do. So the ghost is a kind of "pres/absence," there but then again not there, the source of a general disturbance in the present. So if we think of education on a hauntological model, as visibly present yet also visibly disturbed, it is because, on the premise of a hauntology, it is haunted by the event. The event is the ghost in the machine (computers, overhead projectors, buildings, offices, contracts, etc.), a machine for producing events, if that were possible. The spectral effect of the school is to leave students disturbed and provoked, believing in ghosts they never believed possible, never imagined were real. By the time we are done with them, they will never be the same. Their lives will be destabilized; they will have lost their equilibrium. They will see ghosts everywhere. Everywhere questions, suspicions, longings, doubts, dreams, wonders, puzzles where once peace reigned. Nothing will be simple anymore. They will never have any rest. We have come to bring the hauntological sword, not the peace of presence. So it is of central importance to clarify what I mean by the event and its spectral qualities.

Let us begin by saying that the event, like any ghost worthy of the name, is not what visibly happens but *what is going on invisibly in what visibly happens* (Deleuze 1969, 149). It is not what is palpably present, but a restlessness with the present, an uneasiness within the present. Something disturbs the present but we do not know what it is — that is the event. Something is "coming" (*venire*) to get us but we don't know what. What is that if not a ghost?

The event is not what we desire but something haunting our desire (Derrida 1991, 30). The event is not what we desire but what is being desired in what we desire, some deeper disturbance of our desire. When we desire this or that, we have the uneasy feeling that something else is getting itself desired in that desire, like a *desire beyond desire*. In this sense, we can never say what we desire. We do not know what we desire. Still, this is not some fault or limitation in us, a failure on our part to know what we are doing. It is the very structure of the event, of temporality, of the openness of the future, of the ghost of the future.

As you cannot see a ghost, the event is structurally *unforeseeable*, the coming of what we cannot see coming, not because we are shortsighted but because of the spectral structure of the future, of the temporality of the event. There, is of course, a future that we can see coming and provide for, the future of our children or our retirement, which Derrida calls the "future-present." But the event concerns the "absolute" future, the future for which we cannot plan, a future beyond the future, that visits us like a thief in the night, that haunts us in the night. Faced with what we cannot "see coming" (*voir venir*) we do no more than to try to discern its indiscernible demands, as if we were Jacob wrestling through the night with an angel. Vis-à-vis an "absolute" future we are asked to take a risk, to say "Come — and let's see what comes" (*voir venir*).[4]

Over and beyond our completely reasonable expectation of what is possible, over and beyond the sane, visible economies of the world, the event arrives like the possibility of the impossible, of the unforeseeable, of some invisible spirit in which we did not previously believe. The coming of the event is the coming of *the impossible* (Derrida 2007, 43–47). When we are visited by the event it seems as if the impossible has just happened, as if the impossible were possible after all. Is this magic, a miracle? Is this place haunted?

The present is made an unstable, uneasy place, shaken and disturbed by invisible forces, and this is because it contains something with which it cannot come to grips, something *uncontainable*. That is the event, which is contained in what happens but cannot be contained by what happens. The present contains what it cannot contain.

---

4   This Derridean motif is deployed with aplomb in Catherine Malabou, *The Future of Hegel: Plasticity, Temporality and Dialectic,* trans. Lisabeth During (New York: Routledge, 2005).

The event is like a ghost whispering in our ear, making *promises,* like the visitation by some spirit that pretends to know the future. The event is not what happens but what is being promised in and by what happens, enticing us to live on promises. By the same token, if what is being promised belongs to an absolute and unforeseeable future, then this promise comes without guarantees, and nothing protects the promise from the threat of the worst. Not every angel is good; not every spirit can be trusted. Every promise is a *risk.*

But who or what is "making" this promise? If I knew that, Derrida says, I would know everything. He means he would be able to identify the ghost, make it entirely visible and present. The event is not something I do, or something we do, not anything that is being done by someone or something. Do not separate the doer from the deed, Nietzsche says. There is no agent of the event, no active agency that brings it about, which means that the event is carried out in the *middle voice.* In virtue of some mysterious spectral operation, something is getting itself desired in and through and beyond our concrete and particular desires; something is getting itself promised in the particular promises that are all around us. If we could say *who* or *what* is making this promise, then the promise would not be the event, and it would not be a risk, for we would know someone real and substantive stands behind the promise, something backs it up. We would have driven out all the specters, exorcized one ghost too many. When Derrida says "give," abruptly shifting from the aporia of the gift into the performative order, we ask, who is speaking here? Who calls for giving? Who has the authority to make such a call? This call, which is not a command or a direct order, has a certain force, but it is perforce a spectral force, a weak and unforced force, with no army to enforce it. It does not have the force of law but only the weakness of a plea for justice (Derrida 1992, 3–69). Is this the voice of some spirit that somehow and invisibly manages to make itself felt? If we could identify the source, the call would cease to be a call. It would have the force of God or nature, of some super-presence instead of a spectral semi-presence, which we would be compelled to obey under penalty of disobeying God or defying nature. In order to protect the weak, fragile, and uncoercive character of the call, the origin of the call, *s'il y en a,* must be spooky, spectral, and indeterminate. *Es spükt,* it spooks, something spooks, something spooky is going on (Derrida 1994, 172).[5] All that we can say is that this call is made in the "middle voice," without being able to identify an active agent calling. Something is getting itself said and called in a word like "gift" — and how many other words are there like that, words of an elementary but weak force? Some unknown spirit, something, *je ne sais quoi,* comes over us and asks something of us, asks for our faith, asks us to pledge our troth, without pretending to be a law of God or nature. Or perhaps precisely by "pretending" to be God or nature, but even so something is happening in this pretense.

Like any ghost, holy or not, the event does not exist; it *insists.* The event is not an agent, nor an existing visible thing, neither a who nor a what to be thanked or blamed. It is not some identifiable person or object, not "God" or "Being" or "History," not the "People" or the "Party" or the "Spirit," not the "unconscious" or "economics" or the "will-to-power." The event insists in and within what exists, prying open what exists in the name of something unnamable, unforeseeable, a promise/risk beyond our imagining.

The event (*événement*) in the broadest possible sense is the specter of the future (*avenir*), meaning what is to-come (*à venir*).[6] The event is the *to-come itself,* if there were such a thing, which there is not, since the event is not a visible palpable thing, not what happens, but what is going on invisibly *in* what happens. Deconstruction is situated at the point of exposure of the present to the to-come, precisely when the present feels the pressure of the "to come," which is an infinite or infinitival pressure. The present is thereby pushed to its breaking point, where

---

5   This general hauntological effect of *es spukt* bears an uncanny resemblance to the general effect of Heidegger's *es gibt.*
6   Permit me to refer to my "Temporal Transcendence: The Very Idea of à venir in Derrida," in *Transcendence and Beyond,* eds. John D. Caputo and Michael Scanlon (Bloomington: Indiana University Press, 2007).

what happens bursts open under the pressure of what is coming. This burst, this deconstruction, this auto-deconstruction is not destruction. To deconstruct is to unsettle and de-sediment, to disturb and haunt, but it is not to smash to smithereens. Quite the opposite, it restores to things the future from which they were blocked by the present. The event insinuates itself into and unsettles what seems settled, insists within what exists. But the force of the "to-come" is a "weak force," like a spirit speaking in the middle voice. There is no identifiable agent behind it, no Big Other, as Žižek would say. It has no police, no army to back it up.

One of Derrida's favorite examples of an event, which is not simply an example, but something close to its heart, is "democracy," a spectral shape which never is what it is, is never what is present (Derrida 2005, 37).[7] At any given moment, no existing democracy can respond to what we call for when we call (for) "democracy," even as we never adequately respond to what democracy calls for. Democracy is always and structurally coming, always to-come. Democracy is the event that is being promised *in* the word "democracy," what *insists* in this word, what calls to us before we call for it, what addresses us, haunts us day and night. "Democracy" is a call, not a state of affairs, an infinitival weak imperative, not a sturdy noun or stable nominative.

Teaching the Event

How can we bring about the event? The very attempt to bring about the event would prevent the event. It breaks in upon us unforeseen, uninvited. Still, there is a certain conjuring of the event, a certain dark art of requesting an apparition. It is possible, Derrida says, to be inventive about the eventive, playing on the old sense of both the Latin *inventio* and the French *invention,* to both invent and discover or come upon. We must

---

7 Derrida had the kindness to refer to my "Temporal Transcendence" in *Rogues,* 37.

be inventive in order to allow its in-coming (*in-venire*).[8] That means getting over a fear of ghosts, being willing to live with strange noises in the night, being hospitable to spooks. It means conjuring the spirits that keep the system open to the event, that keep the system in play, embracing the spooky effects of a quasi-transcendental disequilibrium, living in an elusive state of instability, in a word, a magnificent word coined by James Joyce, "chaosmic," meaning a state that is neither chaos nor cosmos. Either pure order or pure disorder would prevent the event. When Derrida calls this "deconstruction," he invites the misunderstanding of radical chaos, implying that he is out to raze institutions instead of merely meaning to spook them. He is not recommending pure anarchy or a libertarian anti-institutionalism; he has in mind a positive idea of institutions as a scene of the event. Deconstruction is all about institutions — schools, hospitals, political bodies, courts, museums — and how to keep them in creative disequilibrium without tipping over, how to spook their complacency with the promise/risk of the future. What is truly destructive is the opposite of the event, which is the absolute exorcism of the event by the "program," absolute foreseeability, deducibility, rule-governed activity. When the "program" is in place, what happens is a function of the laws of the system, of a rigorous logic, not of the aphoristic, metaphoristic, grammatological energy of the event. The only possible program is to program the unprogrammable, the unforeseeable. Otherwise the ghost or spirit of the event will have fled the premises.

All the aporias surrounding justice and democracy, education and the gift, are problems of the event. All the problems of teaching, of what Gert Biesta calls "subjectification," are aporias of the event, of becoming a subject of the event, of responding to the call of the event — ever since Socrates tried to figure out a way to make students (the patients) the agent of their own instruction, to figure out how students could come to see for themselves, to be struck by the event, instead of simply being

8 This double sense of invention is explored by Derrida throughout *Psyche*, ch. 1.

stung by Socrates; ever since Kierkegaard tried to get existing individuals to assume responsibility for themselves, without being responsible to Kierkegaard (Biesta 2013, 4–5). The teacher must somehow allow the event to happen without standing between the student and the event, without attempting to manipulate the event. The teacher must figure out how to be a weak force, how the middle voice works, how to be an agent without agency, a provocateur who is not an agent, how to engage the spooky dynamics of a haunting spirit.

What is the spectral effect that takes place in teaching? According to the hauntological principle we should say, the event in education is not what happens but what is going on in what happens. What happens is teaching, the schools, but something is going on *in* what happens, something desired with a desire beyond desire, something unforeseeable, something impossible, uncontainable, something coming in and as an absolute future. When this or that is taught, that is what is happening, but the event is what is going on in what happens, which we cannot get our hands on, cannot master or manipulate it, cannot make it happen, but only conjure up. The event is a matter of "indirect" communication, Kierkegaard would say; the teacher is only a midwife of the event, Socrates would say. Teaching does not directly handle the event. It deals directly with the various disciplines, the fields of study, more or less standard form academic operations. But all along, running quietly in the background, is the event. Teaching takes place under the impulse of the event, letting the event be in the teaching, letting it *into* the teaching, letting the event by which the teacher is touched touch the student, so that both the teacher and the student are touched by a common event. But the event belongs to an absolute future that no one sees coming, over which neither teacher nor student has disposal, what neither one knows or foresees or commands, where we do our best in an impossible situation to see what is possible, to "see what comes." It is the invisible, unidentifiable, undetectable operations of the event that has assembled teacher and student together, placed them in the same room, both in the service of the event, *me voici*, in the accusative, in response to the event, in answer to the fetching call of some unknown spirit.

Contrary to the received opinion, there are no masters in the school. The teacher, then, is variously the effect of the event, the caretaker of the event, its *souffleur*, its conjurer, but not its master. The student comes under the spell of the event, is spooked by its uncanny operations, is unaware that some spectral force is afoot in these halls. The school must be the space in which the event is possible, the scene in which every possible scenario of the event, of all the events, imaginable and unimaginable, might take place. To define teaching by the event is to situate the teacher at the point where the present is spooked by the future, trembles with the specter of the to-come. Teaching occupies the cracks and crevices in the present where the present is broken open by some coming spirit. The students are the future, the future we do not see, either because we never see them again, or because they are the future generations which outlive us, so that whatever gifts we have given are given to a future in which we will never be present, an absolutely spectral future in which we will be but shades.

But if education is what happens, what is the event that is going on? If it is a spook, does the spook have a name? Which spook do I have in mind? Education is one of the openings of the event, one of its thresholds, one of the places the event takes place. But what is the event of education (if there is one)? There is, of course, no one event, no event of all events, for that would lead to terror. Events disseminate, spread rhizomatically, by contamination, intimation, indirection, association, suggestion, by chance. Otherwise we would reinstate the old theology of sovereignty, the old top-down onto-theological order, the metaphysics of the program, of mastery, of which the omnipotence of the good old God would be the paradigm — the old order of the king, of the father, of the master, to which the "school-master" belongs. Were we to allow a theology into this scene, it would not turn on the sovereignty of God but on the chance for grace, for the event of grace, for the grace of the event, for which the classroom attempts to provide the scene.

Still, what is the distinctive call or address that takes place in the school, the spirit that haunts the halls of the school? To think the event that takes place in the school, which is what I am proposing to undertake, and which is what this association calls the "philosophy of education," is to ask what is promising, what is being promised in the middle voice by the "school," where the school joins the list of words of elementary promise, words that tremble with the quiet power of the promise, the quiet power of the possible. What is getting itself promised in "education," the "university," the "school?" What spirit is calling to us in what we call a "school," a "university," a "teacher," a "professor?" Whoever enters the spectral space of the school is answering a call, responding to some spirit calling us together here in common cause. What calls? What does it call for? Who is being called upon? To what future does it call us forth?

If I were to throw all caution to the winds, to attempt in an act of sheer folly to condense the event of which the school provides the scene, to name this spook, I would say the school is the place where, in an effort to let the event happen, we reserve the right to ask any question. The school is mobilized by a spirit calling—give, ask, question, open up, risk—to put anything and everything into question, even and especially every sacrosanct thing like "God" or "democracy," or what we mean by "reason," "knowledge," "truth," which are among our most intimidating, risky and promising words (Derrida 2004, 129–55). It may well be the case, for example, that what is being promised in the word "democracy" will come at the cost of the word "democracy," which may finally prove itself to be an obstacle, a way to prevent the event. For after all, if the "democracy to come" is unforeseeable, how do we know it will still be a "democracy?" When he was once asked this very question, Derrida responded that, in the expression "the democracy to come," the "to-come" is more important than the "democracy" (Derrida 2002, 182). So then the school will be the place that puts democracy into question, in the very name of what democracy promises. The school is the assembly of those who answer the imperative or the call of the school—dare to ask, to question, to think, dare to know, dare to teach and dare to learn, dare to put what we think we know at risk, dare the event to happen.

What I am saying at this point is conjuring up the old and venerable spirit that inspired the Enlightenment, *sapere aude,* dare to know, but I am saying it in the spirit of a new enlightenment, which is enlightened about any (capitalized) Enlightenment, which understands that there are many lights and that enlightenments come in many versions. This new enlightenment is not afraid of the dark; indeed, it begins with the recognition that the absolute future is in the dark. This new enlightenment is not afraid of the ghosts which the old Enlightenment tried to exorcise. It understands that there are other things than light, that the event is not only a matter of light. So in saying "the right to ask any question," I am not proposing a one-sidedly cognitive ideal, emphasizing the light of the idea. The event is not only cognitive light and not primarily something cognitive. I have said the event is something that I desire with a desire beyond desire, so that the event has an erotic force; and I have said that it calls and solicits me, so that it has a "vocational" force, provoking me, evoking my response, transforming my life. The general effect of specters is to inspire, for better or for worse.

The teacher has to play the delicate role of conjurer, of indirectly calling up an elusive spirit, of letting the event be, and that is because to learn is to be struck by the event. To teach is to teach by way of the event, to let the event touch the student. Teaching is haunting, subtly intimating that there are spectral forces afoot. That involves conceding the common exposure of the teacher and the student to the event, that there are unknown specters all around, and that we share a common situation of non-knowing and mortality and open-endedness. To teach is to ask a question to which one truly does not know the answer, because no one knows, and to make the answers we all think we know questionable. To teach is to expose our common exposure to the specter of the secret. To learn is to unlearn what we think we know and expose ourselves to the unknowable. Teaching and learning alike are a matter of allowing ourselves to be spooked.

The aporia of the school is to have administrators who do not produce administered institutions and to conduct "programs" that do not program the school, that do not bind and coerce the event. That means the program must be in-ventive, which means that it lets something break in, so that in the end no one, neither the planners nor the implementers of the program, can know exactly where it will lead, but no one is afraid of the risk. The program is not meant to program. It must be inventive in the double sense: as carefully planned as possible, but also designed to inject the system with chance, to allow entry to the aleatory spirits and the spooks that haunt the system, to "see what comes," so that the "program" is "designed" to deal with a future that we cannot design. The school is a place of uncanny and unnerving instability, preserving a space of openness, a readiness for the future, pushing forward into an unknown future. All its ideas and ideals are all spooks, both shadowy specters of the past and faint images of an unforeseeable future. In the school, things are placed and displaced, posed and deposed, venerated but also innovated, respected but also subjected to the infinite, infinitival pressure of the to-come. Whatever has been constructed is deconstructible, and whatever is deconstructible is deconstructible in the name of what is not deconstructible, and what is not deconstructible is a spook, a specter, neither present nor absent, a promise, still to come, the to-come itself, the absolute future — of the school, of the teacher, of the student, of us all, of the earth.

All of the aphoristic and even anarchic energies of deconstruction, all its impishness and seeming impudence, which seem mistakenly to some as sheer relativism, are like angels tending to the arrival of some unknown event while displacing the forces that would prevent the event. This does not pit deconstruction against systems, institutions, orders, in short, against economies of one kind or another, which are after all the only thing that exists. But we are here today because we are not satisfied with what exists and because we are haunted by what *insists*. Deconstruction is a style of displacement, a way of haunting these systems by inhabiting them from within, keeping all the inhabitants slightly off balance, in a state of optimal unease and disquiet, which lets events happen. The event is what allows invention, inventiveness, and reinventability, effecting a well-tempered dis/order. The event is the resistance offered to a closed system, to a program, meaning everything run by rules so that nothing is unruly and there are no surprises. The love of order in the end is too powerful, too overwhelming, and it must be resisted by the order of love.

This hauntological operation is repeated every time a deconstructive analysis is undertaken. The "gift" is what disturbs the economy and prevents it from devolving into a *quid pro quo* system of exchange. "Justice" is what haunts the law, keeping it appealable and repealable, without which the law would be a monster. "Forgiveness" is what keeps the moral order from descending into a closed cycle of retribution. "Hospitality" is what keeps the system of privacy and property from shutting out the stranger, the figure of which for Levinas is the door which both closes and opens. In every case the event haunts the system with the specter of its future, which also means to assume the risk of having a genuine future, which is a real risk. Nothing says this will not have been an evil spirit, that the event will not be a disaster, that we will not in our attempt to reinvent ourselves expose ourselves to the wolves of the worst evils. The rules are a way to play it safe, but if the rules overrule the event, then to play it safe is to risk the loss of the event. Safety is dangerous; everything is dangerous.

Accordingly, I reimagine my haunting spirit not as an omnipotent God but as a weak force, a quiet call, an invitation, a solicitation.[9] This God is not a "necessary being" but a maybe, a "perhaps," whose "might" is the subjunctive might of the might-

9 As Gert Biesta says, "But if subjectivity is an event, something that occurs in a domain 'otherwise than being,' then it follows that strong education has no role to play here because in a very literal sense it cannot 'reach' the event of subjectivity. In relation to subjectification, to the event of subjectivity, there is nothing for education to produce. This is why in relation to subjectification we need an idea of the weakness of education and of education as a weak, existential force, not a strong metaphysical one." Biesta kindly makes

be it whispers in my ear. Perhaps the name of the event that takes place in teaching, the name of the spirit that haunts everything that is going on in teaching, is nothing more or less than the spectral workings of "perhaps." Perhaps we require a pedagogy of weakness, of the "weakness of the school," of the university, as the place whose suppleness and plasticity allows the event to take place, allows the promise, the "perhaps" to take place. Perhaps the very idea of the event is this "perhaps," to expose ourselves, teachers and students alike, to the quiet power of "perhaps," the weak force of "perhaps" that steals over unawares everything that passes itself off as "present." Perhaps, the event that takes place in the school is to let the subtle and oblique energies of the "perhaps," of possibilities hitherto unimagined, slip in like a fog and make everything tremble with a future we cannot see coming. Perhaps, the ghost that scares us the most is the soft voice of "perhaps."

Conclusion

When teachers threaten to "work the contract," they engage in a hauntological exercise. They are trying to spook the world by holding up a mirror to the world so that it can be frightened by its own image and see the meanness of its ways. Moved by the better angels of their nature, they are saying: imagine a world in which we have suspended the gift, prevented the event, banished all the invisible spirits that haunt the halls. They spook the world with a vision of what it would be like if the world were all in all, a rigid system of exchange, with no gaps, no breaks, or openings; no ghostly apparitions of something coming, no obscure spirits, no promises, no gift, no grace, and no chance of the event. They are reminding the economy of the world, its institutional forces, that without the gift the world would be a nightmare. The doors of the institution would still be open for business, the computers, the printers, the overhead projectors

an adroit adaptation of my *The Weakness of God: A Theology of the Event* (Bloomington: Indiana University Press, 2006).

would still be there, but the spirits that haunt its halls would have fled. The school would have been absorbed into the *quid pro quo* sanity of the world. The position of the teachers is strategic, an "as if," a "perhaps," here in the form of a perhaps not, like Bartleby's preferring not to. They have been driven to the extreme, forced to act as if there is no event. They are saying, if you want absolutely balanced books, not the gift, if you want an ontology, not an hauntology, if you want to banish all the ghosts, this is what the world would look like: no events, no "perhaps," no future, nothing coming.

REFERENCES

Biesta, G. (2013). *The Beautiful Risk of Education*. London: Paradigm.

Caputo, J.D. (2007). "Temporal Transcendence: The Very Idea of *à venir* in Derrida." In *Transcendence and Beyond*, ed. John D. Caputo and Michael Scanlon. Bloomington: Indiana University Press.

Deleuze, G. (1969). *The Logic of Sense*, trans. Mark Lester et al., ed. Constantin V. Boundas. New York: Columbia University Press.

Derrida, J. (1991). *Given Time, 1: Counterfeit Money*, trans. Peggy Kamuf. Chicago: Chicago University Press.

———. (1992). "The Force of Law: 'The Mystical Foundation of Authority,'" trans. Mary Quantaince. In *Deconstruction and the Possibility of Justice*, ed. Drucilla Cornell et al. New York: Routledge.

———. (1994). *Spectres of Marx: The State of Debt, The Work of Mourning and the New International*, trans. Peggy Kamuf. New York: Routledge.

———. (2002). *Negotiation: Interventions and Interviews: 1971–2001*, trans. Elizabeth Rottenberg. Stanford: Stanford University Press.

———. (2004). "The Principal of Reason: The University in the Eyes of its Pupils." In *Eyes of the University: Right to Phi-*

losophy 2, trans. Jan Plug et al. Stanford: Stanford University Press.

———. (2005). *Rogues: Two Essays on Reason,* trans. Pascale-Anne Brault and Michael Naas. Stanford: Stanford University Press.

———. (2007). *Psyche: Inventions of the Other, Vol. 1,* trans. Peggy Kamuf et al. Stanford: Stanford University Press.

Malabou, C. (2005). *The Future of Hegel: Plasticity, Temporality and Dialectic,* trans. Lisabeth During. New York: Routledge.

5

The Intimate Schoolmaster and the Ignorant *Sifu*: Poststructuralism, Bruce Lee, and the Ignorance of Everyday Radical Pedagogy[1]

Paul Bowman

Introduction: Unlearning the Crisis

The Pedagogics of Unlearning is an unusual and awkward phrase, for an unusual or awkward formulation. To make my own sense of it I have had to translate it, expand it, and unpack it, in my own way. Inevitably, there are other ways and other translations. But to me, the phrase or formulation "the pedagogics of unlearning" (as the title of this conference) seems to be asking to be translated as something like: "This conference seeks to be about how to emancipate ourselves from everything we ever thought we knew about the logics of teaching and learning." Or, to unpack this more fully: "This conference seeks to be about (a *good thing* called) how to emancipate ourselves from (a deluded condition vis-à-vis) everything we ever thought we knew about

1   My thanks go to two readers of a draft of this paper: Tony Carusi of Massey University and Richard Stamp of Bath Spa University.

(an implicitly bad or at least suspect thing or group of things, at least to the extent that we need to unlearn it or them, called) the logics of teaching and learning."

But does this mean that the conference theme is therefore about establishing how to be great teachers and how to facilitate the best learning? I don't think so. Moreover, there are already plenty of conferences and publications about that sort of thing; and they certainly aren't organized by such an awkward and unusual formulation as "the pedagogics of unlearning." In fact, I imagine that the phrase "the pedagogics of unlearning" was chosen specifically to signal a distance and difference from conferences concerned with "teaching and learning." In other words, it looks to me like there's a deliberate inversion and twisting involved here, which means that even if we are *also* interested in ditching the worst and keeping the best when it comes to pedagogy, we need to maintain this difference in orientation *as* a difference in orientation.

So, what do I think this conference formulation is asking us to do? I think that it is asking us to interrogate all of the key nodal points and rhetorical, conceptual, and ideological coordinates that implicitly and explicitly organise the constellations of thinking, theorizing, and discoursing on pedagogy — whether dominant or conventional, folk or professional. Why might this be important? Is it "merely philosophical" or "entirely academic"? Maybe, yes; but also, such interrogation could come to challenge, reorient or reconfigure pragmatics and pedagogics in any number of ways. Which could be good.

Yet wouldn't this simply be another way of saying that this conference seeks to be about how to "unlearn" the worst in teaching and learning practices? And if so, why this awkward tarrying with the negative? After all, to cut to the chase: doesn't *everyone* want to come up with the *best* pedagogics, the best forms and contents of teaching? I think so. And for any number of reasons. However, when it comes to a consideration of formal education — in schools, colleges, and universities — this matter seems incredibly overburdened by a very familiar argument, which runs something like this: *matters of teaching and learning matter because education matters, and education matters because its forms and contents (but more importantly its values) help to produce certain kinds of people, certain sorts of subject, and hence it matters for the very fabric of society.*

As many have argued: contemporary governments more and more regard the school as both the focus and the method, the target and the paradigm, the concept and the field for implementing not just educational policy, but policies of all kinds. It is as if educational institutions are there purely to be tinkered with — as if they are machines to be manipulated, in order to produce a regularised, predictable product (*subjects*), like sausages from a sausage factory. In other words, education is effectively regarded as an ideological state apparatus. And, today, you don't have to be an Althusserian to think this. Indeed, the belief that educational institutions are incalculably important, politically and ideologically, is something that everyone — from the most conservative to the most radical of thinkers — seems to agree on. This is why it so easily seems so logical to want to get rid of (or to unlearn) the bad and to institute the good. What other reason for this conference could there be?

I can think of at least one other possibility. Maybe we need to unlearn this very argument; to disarticulate the presumed homogenizing connection between pedagogy and politics; perhaps in order to "save" what Derrida called the "hospitality" or the promise of the "openness" of the university in the face of generalized ends-and-outcomes-oriented managerialism. If we could uncouple the connections that have turned all educational contexts into little more than the crucibles, laboratories, and fields of educational policies, then this could in itself be radical and transformative. Such would seem to be part of the rationale for this conference.

Certainly, state education seems overburdened with all kinds of policy baggage. And, on the one hand, this seems like a bad thing. But, on the other hand, to reiterate, as I have already proposed, I think that, by and large, we all tend to assume that education is always and already *inevitably and necessarily* a key battleground of and for hegemonies of all kinds. Certainly, we all have certain axes to grind and certain horses that we back. Hence, we do or we don't want creationism or evolution to be taught in schools, and we do or we don't want multiculturalism championed or denounced, and we do or we don't want the learning of facts by rote, and we do or we don't want the encouragement of free critical thinking, and so on.

So far, so paternalistic. However, the real problem for academics seems to arrive when all of this arrives or returns to knock on our own door — specifically, the departmental doors of our own university — when we perceive the presence and force of hegemonies working (or trying to work) *on us,* and we feel the forces of dictates other than those of our own axes and our own horses, it strikes us as outrageous, and we come over all Kantian: the university should be free, we say; and we denounce either the politicization or the depoliticization of the university; and we want to change it, or halt it; even though, in a sense, we are merely experiencing what we say we already knew: the fact that educational institutions are key locations in any kind of hegemonic bloc or formation. It's only that we feel we should be exempt — because we are the philosophers, not the poor, or the uneducated, or the children. Or, if we *can't* be exempt, if we have to be included, we dislike this because this is not the hegemony we would prefer. If it were the hegemony we wanted, then we'd think we were free. But it's not, and we don't like it, so we say it's a "crisis" and we want to police the crisis, or ward off the crisis, perhaps through the magical alchemy of polemic and critique.

Unlearning Emancipation

But maybe things have already gone too far. Or maybe it's just that I have already gone too far. Maybe my translation of the title "the pedagogics of unlearning" need only be rephrased as a question; perhaps like this: how do we rid ourselves of the instituted delusions of what Jacques Rancière called the "explicative order," and rid ourselves of all of the deleterious consequences of various kinds of pedagogy, from the stultification of individual souls to the generalized maintenance of inequality?

This is a Rancièrean question, of course; or one that I have forged using some of the terms that Rancière uses. Furthermore, my translation-interpretation of the conference title and general field of problematics to be engaged is clearly Rancièrean too. This is because I recognized in the awkward phrase of the title the presence and effects of a reading of Rancière's book, *The Ignorant Schoolmaster*. Plus, I found out that Professor Rancière was to be our closing keynote. So I put two and two together, ignored all the other prompts in the conference "irrationale"[2] to think about this in Lacanian or Derridean terms, and came up with my present translation-interpretation.

So: regarding my Rancièrean question about whether we can rid ourselves of stultification and inequality by education; the short (Rancièrean) answer would be no: No, we can't get rid of these things; we can't rid ourselves of stultifying pedagogy, and we certainly can't eradicate inequality. Not *en masse*. Not institutionally. Not through policy. As Rancière writes at the start of *Education, Truth, Emancipation*:

> there is no social emancipation, and no emancipatory school. Jacotot strictly distinguishes the method of emancipation, which is the method of individuals, from the social method of explanation. Society is a mechanism ruled by the momentum of unequal bodies, by the game of compensated inequalities. Equality can only be introduced therein at the price of inequality, by transforming equality into its opposite. Only individuals can be emancipated. And all emancipation can promise is to teach people to be equal in a society ruled by inequality and by the institutions that "explain" such inequality. (Rancière 2010: 9)

Only *individuals* can be emancipated, argues Rancière. But you can't *institute* this. You can't *bottle* it. You can't *standardize* it. It demands both an *intimacy* (that no social planning or policy or

---

2 The Conference "Irrationale" is here: http://www.unlearningconf.com/irrationale/

instituting can guarantee) and — if schooling is needed — you need *an ignorant schoolmaster*. What is an ignorant schoolmaster? Rancière is not coy about this:

> The ignorant schoolmaster — that is to say one who is ignorant of inequality — addresses him or herself to the ignorant person not from the point of view of the person's ignorance but of the person's knowledge; the one who is supposedly ignorant in fact already understands innumerable things. (Rancière 2010, 5)

In other words: Rancière constructs an *intimate* pedagogical relation, and an *egalitarian* one. Emancipatory pedagogy proceeds on the basis of an assumed equality. It says: if you don't know, work it out; you know how to work things out: so, try. The pedagogue's job is to say, come on, work it out, I want you to solve this riddle; and I intend to verify that you have done it. Famously, Rancière argues that the emancipatory relation still involves *will dominating will*. We do not all become laissez-faire hippies. But, crucially, the pedagogical relation is not to be perceived as one of knowledge versus ignorance or intelligence versus stupidity. These latter interpretations of the pedagogical scene are, in Rancière's terms, *stultifying*. As he writes:

> Jacotot did not see what kind of liberty for the people could result from the dutifulness of their instructors. On the contrary, he sensed in all this a new form of stultification. Whoever teaches without emancipating stultifies. And whoever emancipates doesn't have to worry about what the emancipated person learns. He will learn what he wants, nothing maybe. He will know he can learn because the same intelligence is at work in all the productions of the human mind, and a man can always understand another man's words. (Rancière 1991, 18)

Now, it deserves to be mentioned: this is not just any old argument. Rather, this argument has a central place in Rancière's work. That "a man can always understand another man's words" is arguably a premise central to all of Rancière's political thinking (Rancière 1999). And nowadays, people ("Rancièreans") feel confident with this argument. But, I would like to note that in *The Ignorant Schoolmaster,* Rancière immediately continues this paragraph with a quick anecdote:

> Jacotot's printer had a retarded son. They had despaired of making something of him. Jacotot taught him Hebrew. Later the child became an excellent lithographer. It goes without saying that he never used the Hebrew for anything — except to know what more gifted and learned minds never knew: *it wasn't Hebrew.* (Rancière 1991: 18)

This is a very provocative passage. It is also problematic. It is in a way central to what I want to think about in this paper. However, before I move on to that, I have to add, first, that in order to think about all of this in terms of "the pedagogics of unlearning," we need to remember two things about *The Ignorant Schoolmaster.*

Knowledge of Ignorance

The first is that Joseph Jacotot was *already* a popular teacher, before he "discovered" *anything* about pedagogy. The second is that what he discovered or realized is that you can teach people stuff that you don't know; and/or, in reverse, that you can learn without being taught. So, when Jacotot taught the son Hebrew, what most likely happened was that he told the son to go off and learn Hebrew. Or maybe he even supervised him — in the sense of making sure *that* he was studying, rather than checking *what* he was doing while he was studying. Because, remember, Jacotot wasn't teaching in the sense of imparting or communicating knowledge. He was merely encouraging, inspiring, or insisting that study take place, without policing the method or the result.

Of course, the fact that the boy studied Hebrew but never really learned Hebrew yet nevertheless learned *something,* so much so that it may have helped him to go on to become a lithographer (if there is actually a connection here), is deeply *interesting*. Artists and educators of all sorts have been inspired by this kind of story. It seems extremely upbeat and enabling. But something bothers me about it. It is the fact that Rancière allows the son to know that he does not know Hebrew. What bothers me about this is that Rancière thereby maintains a stability in the relation between knowledge and ignorance. The son *knows* that what he has learned when studying Hebrew was not Hebrew.[3]

This allows Rancière to convey very clearly — as if with a wink and a wry smile — his polemical lesson about pedagogy. *Study stuff; you'll learn stuff; it might not be what it says on the tin, but it's still stuff, and it'll do you good.* Yet, in both its implicit affirmation of the production of "other knowledge" and of the emancipation of the son through his learning of the fact that he can learn, as an equal, the story eliminates an important element of undecidability. It keeps everything in its proper place: ignorance and knowledge. No one in the story knows Hebrew, but the son gains an emancipating sense of self-worth and distinction from the knowledge that *other people don't know what he does know, which is that he doesn't know Hebrew.*

It is this dimension of a clear distinction — or indeed partition or distribution — between knowledge and ignorance that interests me. This is because there are myriad contexts everywhere in the world, in life, in different practices and discourses, where the disambiguation of ignorance and knowledge in this way seems impossible. Moreover, the interminable undecidability of ignorance and learning in most places seems hugely functional. This is what every theory of "discourse" is enabled by. It is certainly what subtends postmodern/Lyotardian theories of the

---

3   Richard Stamp has suggested that in putting it like this I have already twisted the way in which Rancière presents the outcome, because Rancière says that the son knew what other "more learned" minds "did not know," which in the original French is "à savoir *ce qu'ignoreraient toujours* les intelligences mieux douées et plus instruites." Accordingly, notes Stamp, the original maintains that double sense of "never knowing" and "always ignoring."

"legitimation crisis in knowledge." It is, in other words, something of a fact of life.

Segue: Daydream Believing

In this light and from this position, in what follows I want to consider a few more contexts which might help us to interrogate the terms of our most common discourses of and on pedagogy. However, I won't take any of my examples from the realms of either the school or the university. This is because I think to do so would allow us to indulge in our easiest poststructuralist fantasies about the ideal-typical pedagogical scene.

The poststructuralist fantasy about the ideal-typical pedagogical scene is neither "arboreal" nor "rhizomatic" nor virtual nor mediated; rather, it is basically a fantasy about a really great literature seminar. So I want to stay as far away from this fantasy image as possible.

I want to stay away from it for lots of reasons. But now that I've mentioned it, I suppose I am obliged to give some kind of explanation. So, one reason is this: to me, too much poststructuralist thinking and writing about learning still seems based on at best an overvaluation of and at worst a "repressive hypothesis" involving modernist literature — as if the evil instrumental rationality of the world has really got it in for the heroic minority still invested in the saintly endeavour of reading really difficult literature. But what happens if we broaden our frames — or even invert and displace them — in order to think about pedagogical scenes and relations that are rather far removed from the school or university classroom?

If we think about pedagogical scenes and relations that differ from the "wordy," "logophiliac," or indeed "logocentric" preoccupations that tend to be preferred by poststructuralist thinking about pedagogy, it would seem reasonable (surely, even overdetermined) to include practices of the body.

Intimate Lee

Now, I have argued before that an excellent case to consider when thinking about teaching and learning in terms of Rancière's arguments about emancipation and stultification is none other than Bruce Lee. As I argued in a piece I wrote for Michael O'Rourke and Sam Chambers in their *Borderlands* journal issue "Jacques Rancière on the Shores of Queer Theory," Bruce Lee actually proceeded in a very Jacototian manner (Bowman 2009). Moreover, and more importantly, he was not alone. But he also blazed a trail. And this seems important: to borrow and mangle a phrase: others followed — without following.

Bruce Lee was very much an autodidact; he was iconoclastic, hands-on, inventive, verificationist. He was also the author of a massively influential magazine article called "Liberate Yourself from Classical Karate" (Lee 1971), which argued (in effect) that most martial arts pedagogy insists on, produces, and intensifies *deference, reverence,* and *conformity,* via the institution of hierarchies, and hence feelings of *inferiority* and *inequality*. Martial arts pedagogy produces robots, he argued. It stultifies. And it does so because true insight into what he called the truth and reality of combat cannot and should not be institutionalized in the ways it has been. Think of classes of white pyjama-clad students standing in rows performing rote drills of kicks, punches and blocks upon the shouted commands of the instructor. As a counter-image to this, Lee fantasized the figure of the founder of a martial art. He characterizes this figure as fluid and dynamic, as able to move freely and to honestly express himself. The problem comes, he argues, when this figure's followers try to capture the essence of the genius and insight of the master; or indeed, when he or anyone else tries to formalise it. It is at this point of formalization that everything goes wrong. The genius is lost in the very effort to preserve it. This is because the genius of any martial art could be said to lie not in the accumulation of its techniques but rather in the ability to actualize its meta-principle in a potentially infinite array of singular circumstances. In other words, to go beyond Bruce Lee's thought, for a moment: it is because there is no master.[4]

Nevertheless, Lee clearly identified with precisely such a founder figure. This would certainly explain his ambivalence vis-à-vis what he himself had been teaching to his students during the final years of his tragically short life. For a long time he had merely taught what he called *Jun Fan Kung Fu* — and, given that Jun Fan was one version of his name, this did not signify a style as such. It just meant "Bruce Lee's kung fu school." However, in 1968 Lee became enamoured of the combination of the Cantonese terms for "stop" or "interrupt" (which in Cantonese is *jeet*) and "hit" (which in Cantonese is *kune*). This is because he believed that the highest aspiration in all martial arts is to block and strike simultaneously — to interrupt another's attack (*jeet*) and to hit (*kune*) simultaneously. So from 1968 Lee termed his "style" *Jeet Kune Do*. As a name, Jeet Kune Do referred solely to his preferred highest principle and aspiration, or his metaprinciple. However, by the time he was becoming really famous, from 1971 onwards, Lee allegedly regretted naming his approach at all, because a name implies an entity, a fixed identity, with a stable form and content, and Lee wanted what he did and what his friends, training partners, and students did, to keep evolving. Shortly before his untimely death in 1973, he even told his senior students to stop teaching completely. The jury is still out about exactly why he did this.

The most ungenerous interpretations suggest that Lee did this because he was worried that because of his growing celebrity his students would be exposed as inferior martial artists, something that would inevitably reflect badly on him. Other interpretations refer to the fact that because his film career had taken off he knew he couldn't devote enough time to this part of his life, so he sensibly shut up shop. But another equally viable

---

4 My thanks to Tony Carusi for provoking this idea, who commented extensively on a draft of this paper. At this point, Carusi suggested that the foregoing passage was crying out for a discussion of the place of Lacanian *transference* here. However, I have decided to defer such a discussion, in order to maintain focus here.

interpretation relates to his thinking about pedagogy. It is his own senior student, Dan Inosanto, who now regularly reiterates this point: Jeet Kune Do, says Inosanto, is something that can be taught, and learnt, but that cannot be formalized, institutionalized, or standardized. It demands an intimacy that no institution can guarantee. You either get it, or you don't. Consequently, Inosanto himself claims that whilst he teaches a range of martial arts classes to anyone, only select individuals are invited or accepted into his Jeet Kune Do classes.

But none of this is radical. Indeed, it bears family resemblances to one of the most traditional of institutions in Chinese martial arts pedagogy: the tradition of the "indoor student." This is a student selected by the master as the one most apt to carry the torch forward, and who is therefore given considerably more (and considerably more private and intimate) attention. We might evaluate this tradition in any number of ways. In Deleuzean terms, it is arboreal. In Derridean terms, it is inseminatory rather than disseminatory. In Rancièrean terms, it may be either stultifying or emancipatory. However, what is clear is that it demands intimacy.

Ambivalent Intimacy

There is an ambivalence in poststructuralism about intimacy. On the one hand, as we see in Derrida's reading of Socrates/Plato, pedagogical intimacy can be phonocentric, metaphysical, dominating, constraining, and so on. But on the other hand, the intimacy implied in the poststructuralist fantasy scenario of a seminar group of close reading and the close discussion of a difficult modernist literary text is sometimes put on a pedestal and raised to the status of being just about the only kind of authentic revelatory event — the only one that poststructuralists seem to know about, anyway. Might this fetish or fantasy be something we should unlearn? In any case, there does not seem to be any of this ambivalence about intimacy in Rancière's work. In *The Ignorant Schoolmaster* we have illiterate fathers coaching their children in learning to read by making them connect the sound of the words of The Lord's Prayer with the marks on the page, and whole classrooms of students learning all manner of sciences, languages, jurisprudence, and legal argumentation without any formal content being transmitted from the teacher or anyone else to them. All that seems required for ignorant schoolmastery is the alchemy of egalitarian address and hierarchy of wills.[5]

But this type of relation is precisely the one that poststructuralism most seems to worry about. However, poststructuralism seems very comfortable with some other types of intimacy. For instance, it demands extreme intimacy with the textual supplement (specifically with the *book*). Yet it is much less comfortable with the idea of intimacy with the pedagogue. Rancière or Jacotot repeats this in a way. Rancière's Jacotot demands an intimacy with the text (or other object, riddle, or problem); but he also

---

5 Yet it seems to me that, according to what is implied in this text about the need for the teacher to impose his will, and for the teacher to have a mode of address that reaches individuals in terms of what they know, then perhaps once we get over and above a certain size of class or number of students, or after a certain kind of distance or delay, the intimacy-effect may disappear or diminish. As we have just heard Rancière say clearly (in a way that reminds me of Morpheus enlightening Neo in *The Matrix*), "[O]nly individuals can be emancipated." Of course, in *The Emancipated Spectator*, Rancière argues from the start that even a univocal mass-mediated film text still addresses us individually — all together, but all alone, as individuals. Nevertheless, unless "ignorant school-mastery" boils down to the issuing of commands, via megaphone, text message or YouTube clip, then it implies a certain *numerical limit*, or indeed teacher–student *ratio*. Hyperbolically put: herein lies a potential Rancièrean ambivalence, ambiguity, or performative contradiction vis-à-vis intimacy. For, this claim about emancipation as individual is made in a *book*; a book that has not only been mass produced and mass disseminated but has also been translated into many languages and even scanned in as a PDF and uploaded to many sites and disseminated freely (albeit illegally) online, and which therefore countless people have now read. But, is Rancière saying that even if we've merely *read* his arguments and lessons on emancipation, then — as distant, non-face-to-face readers — we cannot therefore or thereby be emancipated? Must emancipation be face to face? In which case, why would Rancière waste the words to write the book? Put differently, we might ask: is Rancièrean/Jacototian pedagogy phonocentric and metaphysical in the Derridean sense? Or, in a related register: what is the status of supplementary technologies, such as the book, the DVD, the MPEG or the online video, when it comes to pedagogy, learning, and unlearning?

seems to require a definite *distance* between teacher and student (or between master and autodidact). The ignorant schoolmaster addresses the student as an equal, but also exerts his or her will. There is a definite personal interaction, from instruction to encouragement to verification. But there is an absolute separation between the commander and the commanded. The teaching and the learning both take place autodidactically, without the transfer of signified content from one mind to another.

Teaching without Teaching

There is a great deal of importance in Rancière's treatment of Jacotot's approach. However, if it actually seems *radical* to anyone, I suspect that this is primarily because they haven't been paying attention to everything outside the text. For, once pointed out, we can see precisely such relations *everywhere*. Just think of the sports coach, the drill sergeant, the sparring partner, the parent or grandparent, or indeed the younger sibling, or one's own students. Each of these, in their own way, merely demands that the student learn — or, indeed, as in the case of the grandparent, uncle, aunt, or younger sibling, merely marvels out loud about this or that achievement (Stamp 2012).

Unlike the martial arts *sifu* or *sensei* or master, or indeed the university professor, the sports coach does not necessarily embody or equal the highest level of skill in the activity. The sports coach is someone who drives the student on, with carrot or stick, with challenges or praise, with advice and criticism, and so on. But their charge does not necessarily *learn* anything from them. Similarly, the drill sergeant, for Freud, merely makes the soldiers hate him by being sadistic to them, until they bond together through their shared hatred and then eventually love him as the person who made them what they are. A good sparring partner will simply present you with problems to be solved: their fist will *keep hitting you,* their foot will *keep kicking you,* or you will keep ending up on the floor being choked out unless *you* work out how to solve these problems. And as certain sociologists have shown, the clucking and cooing of the performance of amazement and pride carried out by older relatives can drive children on to greater and greater achievements of self-learning. Doubtless even the Nike slogan "Just do it" has played on a loop in countless people's heads as they force themselves to learn how to go further or faster or better. Similarly, I know for certain that the words and movement-images of Bruce Lee and other cinematic martial artists, from Jackie Chan to Jason Bourne, play out in montage behind the eyes of countless students and teachers of martial arts. One of my sparring partners used to quite audibly make film sound effects noises while sparring.

The sociologist Loïc Wacquant, who spent three years immersed in the world of boxing in the Chicago ghetto, actually depicts the boxing gym as a *habitus-production-and-maintenance-machine* in which everyone and everything is a teacher: the professional boxers are to be emulated; the novices serve as reminders and yardsticks of development; and when the head coach shouts commands or reprimands at *anyone* in the gym, like "what are you doing over there?" or "keep your hands up!," *everyone* in the gym responds, because even if not directed at them personally, such words are of course universal injunctions in the gym, and therefore they are directed at them personally.

We could go on, and come up with different typologies and taxonomies of pedagogical relations and scenes, ignorant schoolmasters and stultifying pedagogues, in different realms and registers. But there's no need to do that. My point is merely that Jacotot's "universal learning" is universal because, well, it is at least *very widespread*. It is the artifice of the inegalitarian institution that is the anomaly to be questioned. And, again, neither Jacotot nor Rancière are unique here. Bruce Lee did precisely this in the field of martial arts, as have many others since, and (surely) before.

Learning without Learning

Bruce Lee spawned a movement in martial arts whose imperatives boil down to an anti-institutionalism, on the one hand, and an intimate experimental and verificationist ethos, on the other.

In other words — in its most radical versions — the Bruce Lee message can even be interpreted as: *don't join a school or club; work it out for yourself* (Miller 2000). This is what Bruce Lee did: he walked away from — actively renounced — martial arts styles. By the late 1960s he was saying that he no longer saw himself as practicing Chinese Kung Fu at all (Tom 2005).

But in his renunciation of styles and institutions lies the very problem of Bruce Lee. He never completed the syllabus of the martial art he studied in Hong Kong through his teens (Wing Chun). He went to America when he was eighteen and soon started teaching. As a young hotshot he made a name for himself; and in a context saturated by militaristically trained and sports-focused Japanese and Korean martial arts, Lee's Chinese kung fu performances stood out as something else. It was in the US context, saturated by *katas* and points-based competition, that Lee developed his belief that martial arts seemed to be in a sorry state: Currently, the martial arts are ineffective, he said. They are formal, rule bound, artificial. They are full of strictures, a "fancy mess," a "classical mess," "organized despair." Stultifying (Lee 1971). And so he began to innovate. He maintained the Wing Chun centerline; he added Korean Taekwondo kicks; he adopted the Western fencing stance; he emulated the techniques used by the best boxers with the most powerful jabs; he began learning the grappling, in-fighting and ground fighting of Japanese Jujitsu; he explored the weapons styles of the Philippines. And so on.

But was this done in ignorance or knowledgeably? Can you really dip into a martial art — one whose practitioners insist it takes years to master — and pull out bits and pieces? Are you really able to *evaluate* them? Are you even able to *perceive* them? Certainly, this kind of thing is nowadays easily sent up, as a joke. In the online comedy mockumentary series "Enter the Dojo," Master Ken has devised his own martial art, called *Ameri-do-te*, whose motto is "the best of all, the worst of none."

The question that is endlessly asked about Bruce Lee is: was his new hybrid form a real authentic improvement? Or was it that he could only have had the arrogance to think that *any* martial art needed improving because he had not actually finished the syllabus in any martial art (Smith 1999)? There are stories of Bruce Lee returning to see his teachers and classmates in Hong Kong after he had been training away from them in the US, believing he was progressing on his own. In these stories, we hear that Lee demonstrated how much he had improved. His former teachers and peers, however, believed that he had not improved at all! Indeed, to their mind, how *could* he improve? He hadn't finished learning the syllabus, and so didn't know what he was missing.

Accordingly, in this discourse about Bruce Lee, we see (or I see — because I have been trained to see) a version of the kind of disagreement Rancière had with Althusser — which is a version of the disagreement Rancière had with Bourdieu. In this rendition, Althusser would be in the position of the old masters. Bruce Lee would be the revolutionary student, rejecting the institution and instituting a new one. The conundrum is: do you have to go through the ranks of the institution before you can know enough to legitimately disagree with the institution or to be in a position to contest it legitimately? Is this logical, reasonable, and necessary, or is it an inegalitarian, hierarchical, and possibly even stultifying position? Rancière claims that people like Althusser and Bourdieu implicitly or explicitly held the former position. He himself seems instead to advocate the latter.

In the end, our own decisions about this matter little, because this kind of thing happens all the time in the world, and perhaps nowhere more than in and around martial arts institutions. Schools, associations, and styles are instituted, flourish, fragment, and collapse or reform. Agreeing or disagreeing with it is like agreeing or disagreeing with the weather. There are heresies and there are factions. There are paradigm shifts and revolutions. There are mutations and transformations; there are translators and traitors. There is also the growing perception that all styles and systems are hybrids and bastards, each typically claiming a pure lineage, a completeness, a plenitude and unitarity that is actually only pure in that it is purely ideological. Consequently, unlike Jacotot's printer's son, we are rarely, if ever, in a position to know with certainty whether our Hebrew is or is not really Hebrew. *Your Kung Fu is not real Kung Fu; your Taiji is hippy Taiji, my Taiji is real martial Taiji; yours is a bastardized form, mine is the original and best.* And so on.

Of course, it is easy now to say that we know that the idea of the original, like the idea of the authentic, is a red herring. So perhaps we can adjudicate in terms of better and worse. And this is the time-honoured question of martial arts: which martial art is best? Which martial art works best? Which style would win? Whether or not Bruce Lee really knew the ins and outs of all the other martial arts, was his own construction objectively better or worse than others? Surely *this* can be decided. You'd think. Unfortunately, deciding this is like deciding which is the best move in rock–paper–scissors/scissors–paper–stone. Style against style is only ever person against person in context after context. In other words, interminably undecidable.

Which is perhaps why Bruce Lee never really engaged in polemics against specific martial arts styles. His problem was with the very idea of style, and specifically with the way styles were taught. Styles stultify, he argued. True learning is not about accumulation but about reduction. You have to get to the essence. Hence, he proposed, his approach (Jeet Kune Do), could be taught and could be learned, but could not really be institutionalized. It could not be formalized. It demanded an ethos and an intimacy. It was less about formal content and much more about attitude. Teaching and learning should be experimental, alive, moving, hands-on, verificationist, one-on-one. In learning Jeet Kune Do, Lee argued, one is in a sense only *relearning* — retooling, reorienting, reprogramming, rewiring, rewriting — one's own body. Learning how to "honestly express yourself" is the phrase Lee would often use.

This started in the 1960s. Bruce Lee became world famous in the 1970s. He either initiated or was at least at the forefront of a massive Jacototian revolution in martial arts pedagogy that accelerated from that point on in the West: anti-institutional, inventive, verificationist, intimate, one-on-one, or one-on-two, or one-on-three, and so on. A lot of this inventiveness has proceeded in more or less complete ignorance of classical or formal martial arts disciplines. This anti-disciplinarity has of course produced new disciplines: MMA (mixed martial arts) was — as its name attests — never meant to be one thing. But over time it has become so (kicking, punching, grappling, ground), with recognizable features and forms.

Whence the paradox: the rejection of discipline is not freedom from discipline. All martial arts revolutions, all martial arts paradigms, all martial arts learning, involve retraining one's body, or bodily propensities. This can only happen both through and to the extent that what emerges is a *discipline*. Without the institution of discipline — inherited or invented — you get nothing. No change, no improvement, no event. The discipline can be adopted (like when you join a club); or it can be invented (like when you devise your own style, techniques or training regimen). It will always be implicitly or explicitly social, or invented from socially circulating materials, discourses, ideas, and principles.

Most revolutions in martial arts paradigms and institutions that I know have involved the rejection of one discipline and the reciprocal construction of another. To stick with Bruce Lee: the legend has it that he had a major rethink after ending one challenge match completely exhausted and dejected because he had not won the fight much more quickly and efficiently. Thus, the legend continues, he rejected a lot of the training and techniques specific to the style of Kung Fu he had hitherto practiced, and added weight-training, running, and other stamina training, boxing-style training, and a whole range of pad work and bag work, as well as attention to diet. Some say he also took performance-enhancing drugs.

However, much of the logic and structure of the Wing Chun "nucleus" remained active within his new creation. As Derrida put it, an institution is not just the four walls which surround us; it is the very structure of our thought. And Bruce Lee's thinking about combat can be said to have remained hegemonized by the structure of Wing Chun's implicit theory of efficiency in combat.

Unlearning Discipline

Which raises an interesting question. Can discipline be unlearned? In an obvious sense, yes, of course it can. Lack of practice or improper practice means getting out of practice, getting sloppy, drifting away from the proper, forgetting, getting it wrong. This is as true of spending time away from training as it is for spending time away from academia as it is for not practicing your foreign language or even not practicing drinking your beer. And so on. Indeed, if we follow certain of the implications in Derrida's argument about the inevitability of dissemination, then the question might perhaps be reposed as one of whether it is ever possible to halt the drift and warps and discursive wending away from discipline. As Adam Frank argues in his ethnographic and genealogical study of *Taijiquan* in Shanghai, one need only have a quick read of the so-called Taiji "classics" to realize that the art these 19th-century texts are discussing is very different — very different *indeed* — from anything seen in the parks of Shanghai today. This is because the styles have drifted, bifurcated, intermingled, been subject to fashions, fads, government policies, standardizations, the modernisation movement in the early 20th century, Maoism, and so on and so forth; such that any practitioner of any form of Taijiquan today is literally embodying decades upon decades of writings and rewritings that they cannot but be largely ignorant of. The embodied practice is a material residue of historical layers and all kinds of interventions that are in effect the unconscious of the activity.

On a related tangent, Frank also mentions the problem of the vacuum left in Shanghai's parks after the state crackdown on Falun Gong practice in the 1990s. He notes that in order to fill the spaces where Falun Gong practitioners had previously been, the government actually bussed in hundreds upon hundreds — even thousands — of practitioners of a new "ancient" art, called *Mulanquan*. Now, Mulanquan is passed off as ancient, but its first appearance in public was in the wake of both the crackdown on Falun Gong and the global success of the Disney animation, *Mulan*. Needless to say, surely most of the now myriad practitioners of this sanitized and state approved form are ignorant of its peculiar emergence or institution. It is only thanks to Adam Frank's publication of knowledge gained on his intimate ethnographic research that I have learned this myself. So can I even be sure that I know it? This may be a version of a Lyotardian "postmodern legitimation crisis in knowledge," but it also sums up a problem for anyone who practices what they may want to believe to be an ancient and timeless Chinese or Japanese art: is this the real thing? Is my Hebrew *really* Hebrew? Do I really know Hebrew? Do I really know Taiji? Is what I know *really* Taiji?

Interestingly, most practitioners of Asian martial arts — Eastern and Western practitioners — have not the faintest idea about or interest in the actual history of the art they practice. They may believe all kinds of things about a lineage stretching back to Bodhidharma or Zhang Sanfeng or the Shaolin Temple. But most martial arts are *not allowed* to have a history, in the sense of change or development. And this is not necessarily either a problem of orientalism or self-orientalisation. Rather, it is a matter of what Derrida called *teleiopoeisis*: the crucially important political process of evoking the ancient and unchanging as a proof of the present.

Nevertheless, history moves. Discourses drift. Stabilizations disseminate. Fashions jolt. There is no pure repetition in embodied or kinetic or any other kind of mimesis. There is reiteration, which equals the introduction of alterity. This goes on without our noticing. If we noticed it, we would try to halt it. Because our aim is learning, not unlearning.

But, if it were: could discipline be consciously unlearned, *deliberately* rejected, and with or without a teacher? Can we unlearn the habits of our own lifetime? Can you teach an old dog new tricks? I would propose that learning something new — something truly different — is often likely to involve a reciprocal unlearning. To stay with the example of Taiji: I spent over a decade learning Taiji, after having studied several other martial arts at different times for different lengths of time. The discipline of Taiji demands more or less exactly the *opposite* of everything

I'd ever learned to do before. Learning Taiji involved *unlearning* so many accumulated habits: resistance, force against force, using strength, separation, speed. And I would have to say that this kind of thing could not have been learned by me without a teacher. However, the basic teaching was mimetic. (Hands here, feet here. Watch. Copy.) The more advanced teaching was necessarily tactile and hands on. Error was shown, in terms of what happened to my body (pain, being pinned in an arm lock, or head lock, or throw). Correctness *revealed itself* (in terms of not getting trapped or thrown, or in terms of trapping, locking, or throwing the other). The teacher's words were limited to commands, corrections: relax your shoulder; regain your posture; turn from the waist; yield; push.

Unfortunately, this kind of bodily knowledge is all too easily unlearned. It requires such a high degree of proprioceptive sensitivity and control that if you don't use it, you lose it. You can remember it intellectually; you can discuss it in words; but your body loses the ability to know it and do it.

So anthropologists and sociologists speak of bodily knowledge, embodied knowledge, the intelligence of the body. But I don't think they speak of bodily stupidity or the stupidity of the body. Ignorance, perhaps: bodies can be ignorant. Bodies can not-know, can be unaware; or indeed can ignore. But you are unlikely to hear anyone say (other than in jest) "my body is too stupid to do push-hands," or "my body is too stupid to do a jumping spinning back kick." And you are unlikely to think you are more *intelligent* than your training partners if you beat them in any kind of sparring. You are merely likely to have trained harder, longer, or better. Everyone is equal. Anyone can knock anyone else out. One meaning of "Kung Fu" is simply the disciplined, sustained, skilled investment of time and effort. Every martial arts teacher knows that the distance between teacher and student can close fast, sometimes in an instant. Indeed, arguably one of the basic reasons to teach students is to bring them up to a level where they can push you, to make you keep up your own discipline.

Conclusion: The Pedagogics of Unlearning

In conclusion: Disciplines are invented traditions. The knowledge that disciplines produce is not only disciplinary knowledge but also and perhaps fundamentally knowledge of the discipline. This is as true for academic disciplines as it is for martial disciplines. All have their "reality tests" and modes and manners of verification and self-verification or validation and self-validation. And very often it is possible for even contiguous work in contiguous disciplines to develop in complete ignorance of the work in the other field. This is not because researchers are lazy or stupid. It is rather that the metaphor for disciplinary work itself — specifically, the word "field" (as in "disciplinary field" or "academic field") — is something of a misnomer. This is because, today, at least, so-called academic fields are really rather more akin to halls of mirrors, in which you can see yourself and other objects reflected back at yourself, in various shapes and sizes, but without really knowing where they are, and without being able to see anyone or anything round the corner or reflected away.

Hence my proposal that we might now want to unlearn the argument about pedagogy as a key cog or ideological apparatus in a densely reticulated socio-political terrain. The very dominance in vocational–educational–employment vocabulary of the sacred term "transferrable skills" attests to the fact that education is by and large not immediately connected with anything else anywhere else, without an effort of translation and transformation.

Unlearning disciplinarity may demand what Rancière once called "indiscipline." There is inevitably some debate about what this might mean. I will take one final look at the field of martial arts to see whether academics might learn anything from it. My take on the key feature of the most recent revolution in martial arts pedagogy — initiated by Bruce Lee but elaborated much more fully in various directions in his wake — might be summarized like this: martial arts are to be unlearned because we have to concede that the reality that martial arts seek to master is not unified, univocal, predictable, or masterable. It is not the eminently manageable and manipulable space of the *dojo*, *dojang*, or *kwoon*. Instead, what has to be acknowledged is our ignorance of the chaos, unpredictability, and the traumatic effects of the irruption of the reality of violence. Probabilities can be played with, predicted, estimated, guesstimated — imagined. But, to echo Paul de Man, every answer to every question in the teaching and learning of martial arts, self-defence, or combat skills should really be "perhaps."

The new paradigm is based in the perceived need always to interrupt discipline before it settles down as a system, and settles into the function of, as it were, offering reassurances to children — to borrow a phrase from Derrida. This is exemplified in a spectrum of approaches. On the one hand, there are fighting systems that are based on acknowledging the likelihood of the destruction of most people's training by the chaos and violence of an attack. On the other hand, there are approaches based in psychology, sociology, and certain aspects of biology (specifically around the effects of what some authors call "the chemical dump," or the explosion of often completely incapacitating chemicals within one's body in the event of attack). And so on. What all share is a principled commitment to indiscipline because of the unpredictability of reality and hence the certainty of ignorance — and the power of surprise.

The surprise attack, the surprise of violence — in fact, any surprise — can totally incapacitate anyone. But this is not necessarily negative. Surprises come from everywhere. My final anecdote. When I first began studying Taiji, when my head and heart were filled with mysticism and orientalism and magic, I complained to my Taiji teacher about a steep hill that I could never manage to cycle up without stopping from exhaustion. He said, that's because you are pushing with your legs, but you have to pump from your *dan-tien* (below your belly-button), and then you'll get up the hill and do so without becoming tired at all. So, the next day I tried it. Lo and behold, what he said came true. So, when I next saw him I immediately reported, with delight and pride, that it had worked. He said, "Blimey: so it is true; I've never been able to do anything like that; can you teach me how to do it?"

REFERENCES

Bowman, P. (2009). "Aberrant Pedagogies: Jr, Qt and Bruce Lee," *Borderlands* 8.2, "Jacques Rancière and Queer Theory." http://www.borderlands.net.au/issues/vol8no2.html

Lee, B. (1971). "Liberate Yourself from Classical Karate." *Black Belt Magazine.*

Miller, D. (2000). *The Tao of Bruce Lee.* London: Vintage.

Rancière, J. (1991). *The Ignorant Schoolmaster: Five Lessons in Intellectual Emancipation.* Stanford: Stanford University Press.

———. (1999). *Disagreement: Politics and Philosophy.* Minneapolis: University of Minnesota Press.

———. (2010). "Chapter 1: On Ignorant Schoolmasters." In *Jacques Rancière: Education, Truth, Emancipation,* ed. C.W. Bingham and G. Biesta. London: Continuum.

Smith, R.W. (1999). *Martial Musings: A Portrayal of Martial Arts in the 20th Century.* Erie, PN: Via Media.

Stamp, R. (2012). "Of Slumdogs and Schoolmasters: Jacotot, Rancière and Mitra on Self-Organised Learning." *Educational Philosophy and Theory* 45.6: 647–62.

Tom, T. (2005). *The Straight Lead: The Core of Bruce Lee's Jun Fan Jeet Kune Do.* North Clarendon, VT: Tuttle Publishing.

6

Unlearning: A Duologue

L.O. Aranye Fradenburg & Eileen A. Joy

To Diverge, Rather than to Undo[1]

Probably most of us would agree that, however expert we might become in this or that specialty, we are not richly educated until we have experience of a wide range of disciplines and methodologies — a range that includes critique *and* creativity, analysis *and* immersion, learning *and* unlearning. To our sorrow, this conception of education is rapidly losing favor with the citizenry. There are, of course, pushbacks. San Francisco took to the courts to defend the nature of its City College's (CCSF) course offerings from the so-called "student success" movement, which preaches efficiency and "progress to the degree." The Accrediting Commission for Community and Junior Colleges (a private concern) has tried to shut City College down, and the SF District Attorney has successfully sued to protect it (City Attorney of San Francisco, 2016). Prior to the attack by the ACCJC, CCSF

---

1 Our "duologue" alternates between us, first Aranye, then Eileen, and so on, with some co-composing here and there of an oblique and mysterious nature.

actually maintained graduation rates better than those of most community colleges in the country; the real target of the Accreditation Commission appears to have been the wide range of services CCSF provides for San Franciscans that do not target progress-to-the-degree as such, like the Queer Resource Center, the Women's Resource Center and Library, English classes for recent immigrants, parenting classes for new parents, technical and clerical training, music, painting, and sound engineering. Colleges like CCSF are points of crossover between the academy and the rest of the world. They treat culture shock, give the elderly new leases on life, and resist the ongoing enserfment of the citizenry and those who aspire to it. The "student success" movement means to impoverish sentience, not to enrich it; it's a Thatcherite attempt to discipline and punish, and capitalists love it. But why do so many other people fall for it?

Most students and parents hate teachers, at least some of the time, for subjecting said students to apparently impersonal standards. If we give a student the grade we think they *really* deserve, or if we make them sit for one exam after another, or if we don't even let them into college, then why should we escape external assessment and accountability? If academics play, experiment, muck about with things and other people's money (as opposed to the capitalists who spend many thousand dollars of other people's money on umbrella stands), then we are Žižekian thieves of enjoyment, who wreak havoc in what Lacan called "the dollar zone," ruled by the fantasy of equivalence between and among persons, objects, and symbols. Academic knowledge is edgy, hard to evaluate, and takes a long time to metabolize. Hence, while our new understandings of neuroplasticity and neuronal connectivity make the argument for the value of liberal arts learning, they remain "quiet" in educational policy debates. Arguably, however, the complexification and integration — not homogenization — of brain functions *is* the goal of education.

Educational theorist Wolf Singer strongly emphasizes the roles of connectivity and integration in adult learning: [T]the only major change that nervous systems have undergone during evolution is a dramatic increase in complexity" — that is to say, not only a "massive" increase in the number of nerve cells but also a stunning increase in connections, including "numerous long-range connections" linking "nerve cells that are distributed across remote areas of the brain" (2008, 99). Damasio similarly believes that the experience of selfhood depends on connections between the "primitive" brainstem and the new orbitofrontal regions of the brain (2010, 192–193, 213, 243), and Edelman argues for the role of the basal ganglia in the creation of the redundancy loops that play such an important role in neuroplasticity (2004, 24). A lot that we think is new, or modern, or postmodern, derives from the oldest parts of the triune brain, which participate actively in the "developmental processes in which selection of cortical circuits depends on experience," such that, as Singer puts it, "frequently-occurring correlations in the outer world can be translated into the architecture of connections" (2008, 103). Our environments and histories, in other words, are actually built into the (always changing) functional architecture of our brains. Singer also notes that arousal and attention are required to induce "lasting changes in the circuitry" of the brain; "rewards," hence pleasure, or lack thereof, will be relevant here, as also "behavioral significance," especially since genetic scripts derive from past experience (2008, 105).

Educational researcher Tracy Tokuhama-Espinosa invokes a number of these modulatory and other epigenetic factors in her survey of "major brain functions as they relate to human survival and life skills" — skills that are needed to survive both in academic settings and "social situations." Her list of these major brain functions includes: 1. Affect, empathy, motivation; 2. Executive, decision-making functions; 3. Facial recognition and interpretation; 4. Memory; 5. Attention; 6. Social cognition; 7. Spatial management; 8. Temporal management (2011, 143). These are the same functions that Singer regards as crucial to epigenetic connectivity; they forge the ecological links between brain architecture and worldly experience at stake in both surviving and thriving. As I argue in *Staying Alive* (2013), it's the particular brief of the arts and humanities to enhance the skills on which thriving and surviving depend. We cannot satisfy a "need," assuming we could identify one in the first place, without also experiencing affects and sensations (for example, pleasure, triumph, disgust, shame). So the interconnections of these functions are crucial — for example, the role of affect in decision-making, in focusing attention, and in the formation of memories. Unsurprisingly (as Tokuhama notes), nonverbal forms of communication, like facial expressions and tones of voice, are crucial to effective pedagogy and to the mastery of the abstract symbolism too often thought of as their opposite. These prosodic and *performative* elements are at work in the earliest modes of intersubjectivity, which take place in the context of the attachment process. Indeed, the profound relationality of learning is driven by the affective power of attachment. The psychoanalyst Wilfrid Bion (1959) emphasizes the intersubjectivity of the work of "linking" and "thinking," whereby the attachment figure helps the baby to process chaotic feelings and dread by naming them and connecting them to other experiences. "[T]he brain is a social organ that thrives on interaction with others," as Tokuhama-Espinosa puts it (2011, 166). Learning from other minds is impossible without theory of mind; learning depends on our capacity to understand that other minds are like our own, but also distinct from our own. But theory of mind in turn is acquired in the context of the sensory, affective and aesthetic dimensions of attachment. It is thus a kind of environmental theory, insofar as our awareness of different and non-mindedness depends also on our understanding of what our minds are like.

Tokuhama-Espinosa's suggestion of a link between emotional intelligence and metacognitive capacities (such as reflection) makes perfect sense in the context of attachment behavior in general and "active quiet" in particular. ("Active quiet" refers to the periods of play, e.g., peekaboo, engaged in by young babies and their caregivers, believed to be a chief means of intersubjective learning; these periods are punctuated by restful periods of withdrawal of attention.) Paul Howard Jones, in *Introducing Neuroeducational Research,* also stresses the counter-intuitive importance of metacognitive factors in training teachers of drama. Analysis is not inimical to creativity, he argues; instead, they are mutually supportive brain functions (2010, 138–63). The focused attention and working memory needed for analysis are impossible without affect; associative creativity is rapid and relatively uncensored brain connectivity, as Nancy Andreasen (2006) has argued. Her research suggests that the *corpus callosum,* the thicket of connective fibers linking the right to the left hemisphere of the brain, is specially aroused during times of creativity. Jones's experiments with drama-teacher trainees also emphasize the interactions between right- and left-brain activity (2010, 160). Both hemispheres of the brain are needed for linguistic processing. The left side specializes in syntax and logic, while the right side specializes in the emotional and social significance of utterances. But if the right brain is damaged, the result is not speech that sounds affectless, but rather non-sense, so important are emotional and social contexts in the construction of syntax and logic. And hence the importance of the liberal arts. Scientific method relies on quantitative analysis and controlled conditions; humanistic methods address real-time performance, rhetoric, persuasion, social and emotional expressivity and intelligence, the capacity to improvise. But attention and memory, affect and the senses, are vital to both, and so is relationality. My answer to Malabou's well-known question "What Should We Do with Our Brain?" is therefore "enrich it." The fact is that many basic brain functions must work together to enable even the narrowest of specializations — scientific, mathematical, musical, or otherwise.

How does the concept of "unlearning" illuminate, or question, the neuronal complexity now axiomatic in the new science of the brain? Is there, for example, a "before" to "unlearning," or even an *un* to unlearning? To the extent that the term "unlearning" presupposes a learning that needs to be undone *before* new learning can take place, it conjures a linearity that is not altogether helpful. Here is an example from Descartes: "The chief cause of our errors," he wrote, "are the prejudices of our childhood. [...] I must seriously address myself to the general upheaval of all my former opinions" ([1641] 1955, 23). Here is another example, this time from the discourse of organizational psychology: "[L]earning often cannot occur until after there has been unlearning. Unlearning is a process that shows people they should no longer rely on their current beliefs and methods. Because current beliefs and methods shape perceptions, they blind people to some potential interpretations of evidence […] '[People] […] hold onto their theories until […] failures […] convince them to accept new paradigms'" (Kuhn 1962, cited in Petroski 1992, 180–81; see also Starbuck). Similar narrative elements are at work in the story told by many developmental and psychoanalytic theorists about how our relational expectations — including patterns of anticipation, preparedness, anxiety, hope, and desire — resist modification, producing "entrenchment," or, in the analytic situation, transference. Time lags because the past lives on in us; nothing is altogether superseded. But contemporary fields of knowledge-making are also creating more complex narratives. Not all of us who are psychoanalysts expect our patients to uproot their relational expectations altogether before new ones can begin to form. For that matter, Freud himself characterized all new relationships, including analytic ones, as "new editions," "facsimiles" of old ones. The discourse of unlearning seems on the other hand to polarize the old and the new, where the old simply resists the new, rather than providing opportunities for its creation.

Sameness is not a popular goal these days, and for very good reasons, when it supports the fantasy of eradicating difference. But as so much queer theory has noted, both difference and sameness are relative to larger networks of conceptualization and evaluation. Few things are completely the same or completely different from other things, partly because sameness and difference are in the end relativized abstractions we use to recognize and modify patterns. ("Sameness" is of course not the same thing as a "link" or "linking," but the latter draws on the former.) Abstractions are always cathected, or not, if they have cognitive significance. If the desire for sameness is or can be part of us, is there something in sameness *for* us? Freud precedes his account of the "simplest organism" in *Beyond the Pleasure*

Principle with the paradoxical claim that *staying the same* is the goal of all becoming; we change *because* of our wish for repose, and ultimately, for inanimacy. The "external disturbing and diverting influences" responsible for "the phenomena of organic development" elicit responses that bring about change in the organism, but said responses "are merely seeking to reach an ancient goal by paths alike old and new" (1955, 37–38).[2] By attributing the dynamism of organic development exclusively to the impingements of the external environment on the organism, Freud maintains a distinction between the creature's desire and its ecology that is no longer tenable. But he at least insists that the development of organisms can only be understood in the context of "the history of the earth we live in and of its relation to the sun" (1955, 38). He invites us, further, to suppose "that all the organic instincts are conservative, are acquired historically and tend towards the restoration of an earlier state of things" (1955, 49). It is a paradox worth considering that the drives have a history partly *because* they "tend towards the restoration of an earlier state of things." *Because* the organic instincts are acquired historically, through long ages of experience and reality-testing, and *because* they have been such a long time in becoming, the past is built into them, and they have an allegiance to it. This is a narrative that foregrounds intimacies between sameness and difference, conservation, and exploration. We need, at least, some such story "to reckon with the organism's puzzling determination (so hard to fit into any context) to maintain its own existence in the face of every obstacle": the organism insists on following "its own path to death," and warding off "any possible ways of returning to inorganic existence other than those which are immanent in the organism itself" (Freud 1955, 37).

Here Freud is not so very far from Francisco Varela's use of the term *autopoiesis* to refer to the creature's constant remak-

2   Regrettably, Freud assumes that the "the elementary living entity would from its very beginning have had no wish to change; if conditions remained the same, it would do no more than constantly repeat the same course of life" (1955, 38). Studies of animal innovation do not confirm this assumption about the wishes of living entities. In a way, neither does Freud himself.

ing of itself in accordance with its particular potentialities, affordances, and provisions. Varela conceives of *autopoiesis* as always highly interactive with the organism's environment; it is a systems term, not a term that indicates individual autonomy:

> An autopoietic machine [e.g., a cell], is […] organized […] as a network of processes of production […] of components […] [which], […] through their interactions and transformations[,] continuously regenerate […] the network of processes […] that produced them; and […] constitute [the machine] […] as a concrete unity in space […]. (Maturana and Varela 1972, 78)

Each cell participates in a lavish network of biochemical connections *in order to regenerate* itself as "a concrete unity in space." Autopoiesis resists, not aggregation nor multiplicity, but assimilation to other ways of being alive. What we now know of uterine life is that as soon as we have ears to hear, we hear all the world around us. But we are also born with already-acquired preferences—for the music, the stories, the tastes, and smells of our prenatal experience. Becoming, yes; but becoming is not beyond attachment.

So what is the point of proposing that a linear process must take place—"learning often *cannot* occur until *after*" (my emphasis)—rather than positing that experimentation and its failures are simply part of all "learning" activities (changing, transforming, plasticizing, playing)? For that matter, why would we not posit that experimentation is part of all *living process*? Certainly we can think about habits, ideology, expertise, and the like as "entrenched" materially by the forming of strongly linked neural pathways that then guide us non-consciously. But what does it avail us to think of the process of learning anew as the equivalent of blowing up an old building to make way for a new one? Might it not be possible, that is, to *diverge,* to *re-contextualize,* instead of to undo? To create new, alternative pathways that intersect with old neuronal patterns and thus make creative use of them in the project of living? Is a more holistic thinking possible about the nature of sentient responsiveness?

Particularly if we keep in mind the role of affect in the formation of memories, the question of why we cling or adhere to "tradition" is a matter of affective investments, of cathexis and de-cathexis. It is not clear to me that we can "unlearn" without undergoing mourning. The "giving up" of the old, of "home," in order to make way for the new is one of our most ancient *and* contemporary calls to sacrifice. Freud changed course on this point, acknowledging in a 1929 letter to Ludwig Binswanger that the substitution of an old object for a new one was not an adequate conceptualization since mourning is never really over:

> [a]lthough we know that after [...] a loss the acute state of mourning will subside, we also know we shall remain inconsolable and will never find a substitute. No matter what may fill the gap, even if it be filled completely, it nevertheless remains something else. And actually this is how it should be. It is the only way of perpetuating that love which we do not want to relinquish. (1961, 386)

Studies of creativity show us over and over again that new learning depends on old knowledge. Arguably, the "Renaissance" could not have happened without the critical mechanisms of medieval skepticism, dissent, and iconoclasm. Studies of social learning make similar claims: if the elders in a tribe are wiped out prematurely, the result is not the opportunity to innovate but rather irreparable damage to the tribe's capacity for making and responsiveness. In behavioral ethology, "neophobia" and "neophilia" are not necessarily opposites but more typically interactive elements in always-already ongoing and mutually constitutive vital processes of responsiveness. Even Deleuze and Guattari (1987) argue for the radical potential of "archaisms" in history, just as Jane Bennett (2001) has claimed that premodern materialist understandings of sympathetic bonds and antipathetic lines of flight might inspire "new" respect for the vitality of all things.

How, then, should we think about attachment in the age of complexity theory? "Emergence" seems to resolve so many problems and antinomies. A new open system does not so much reject as reboot on a level of greater complexity the elements of previous systems. Does that mean we can focus on contemporaneity without worrying about the past? It's still with us, so if we work on "us," we're also working on it? And maybe its artifacts, its DNA, can emerge again, chock-full of new significances and material effects that nonetheless could not be were it not for the old ones? We have certainly made arguments like this. "Scale" offers similar opportunities: now we can think about decades, epochs, historical periods, the entire Anthropocene and beyond, as equally legitimate ways of shaping time in the pursuit of certain questions; indeed we can see each "period" as a complex network of different time scales. Foucauldian discontinuism and Foucauldian genealogy perhaps turn out to be the same thing, or complementary (see Fradenburg 2009). The tempting quality of these formulations gives us all the more reason to raise the question of the value of what we learn relative to the value of what we feel (not that these are radically distinct). Do our new-ish ways of thinking ask us to *sacrifice* the experience of attachment, love, bonding, relationality, intersubjectivity, trans-subjectivity? Because all of these involve bonds that do not easily let go. The networks of material relationships always under construction that affect our circumstances (whether at unimaginable distances of time and space or not) are still relationships that have implications for all affective experience. If the sympathies and antipathies that build molecules are an instance of the tendencies to aggregation, symbiosis, *and* autopoiesis characteristic of living process (see, for example, Margulis 1998), on what basis do we assume that our reluctance to change shape is simply an effect of the limitations of subjectivity? What exactly does it avail us to turn irreversible change into higher levels of complexity? What do we lose when we lose lack? In current environmental theory, the soothing, apparently optimistic aspects of the holistic concept of "ecology" (those that tempt us to think everything will adjust somehow — the *Radio-*

active Wolves style of consolation[3]) are cut across by the real tear in the fabric of the Real promised by the current explosion of methane gas from the melting permafrost of the Arctic circle. Not just the polar bears are headed for the slaughterhouse.

Chaos and complexity theory and their offshoots — networks, meshworks, connectivity — dissolve the irreversibility of particular events and actions when and if inspired by melancholy, when "[w]hat should be a thought […] becomes a bad object, indistinguishable from a thing-in-itself, fit only for evacuation" (Bion 1962, 306–307). It is not a good idea to void and avoid lack and discontinuity as intolerable thought-objects, any more than it is to void and avoid continuity and resurgence. The refusal to link and thus think is not the same thing as seeing that a link has been broken. The obsessional defense of *undoing*, like *Radioactive Wolves,* undoes the act(s) of destructivity — our own — which we imagine, not incorrectly, to be the reason for our expulsion from paradise. But if we are expelled together, and there is no "third," if the couple or coupling have already absorbed the "outside" ideas that disturbed the equilibrium of the imaginary, if the damage can be undone one way or another, will they, and we, be all right? Who knows? Obsessional doubt also keeps us *in* the mire of a refusal of attachment, of decision, since, as Sodre puts it of one of his analysands, "any decision represented a loss, and […] this loss was unbearable" (1994, 384). Does unlearning have anything in common with undoing? Or is it an antidote of sorts? Of one thing I am sure: changing people's minds requires empathetic exploration of their *attachments* to prior viewpoints. As Martin Jordan writes,

---

[3] *Radiocative Wolves* is a PBS Nature documentary, released in 2011, that explores how, in the ensuing 25 years after the 1986 Chernobyl nuclear disaster, "forests, marshes, fields and rivers reclaimed the land, reversing the effects of hundreds of years of human development," and how this "dead zone" has become "a kind of post-nuclear Eden, populated by beaver and bison, horses and birds, fish and falcons — and ruled by wolves" (http://www.pbs.org/wnet/nature/radioactive-wolves-introduction/7108/).

> The radical nature of ecology means that everything is interconnected, and it is the job of ecopsychotherapy to help humans negotiate the complex and interdependent present, not by romanticizing the perfect ecological past nor predicting some future ecological catastrophe, but by bearing to stay with the temporal spaces of the complex present. (2012, 145)

I am in complete agreement with the commitment to negotiating "the complex and interdependent present," but not with "bearing to stay [...] in the [...] present." Becoming creates but does not "stay" in spatialized temporalities. To give up yearning, to give up prophecy: why should we give up love, why should we give up fear? The language of "some future ecological catastrophe" dismisses the Real that now screens itself in the form of gigantic methane-releasing sinkholes. Complexity and extremity are not mutually exclusive.

The University-to-Come

Sinkholes are a *drag,* literally. Because they pull the earth out from under your feet and reveal a fact of worldy existence we don't always like to confront: there is no such thing as solid ground, no place you can return to that hasn't changed, or decomposed, or even been eradicated. At the same time, one doesn't easily slip the bonds of history, no matter how changeable that history might be. If current neuroscientific research is right, there *is* such a thing as "transgenerational epigenetic inheritance" (Dias and Ressler 2014), and that means I am carrying around my grandfather's fears and anxieties, maybe even his dreams. In other words, things and situations in the environment that affected my relatives may still be affecting me — behaviorally, neuro-anatomically, and epigenetically. We'll agree, then, that there is no escaping tradition or the past, and likewise, hankering after "the new" (or the "never was") has its decidedly dark side — just think of the Taliban demolishing Buddhist statues in Afghanistan in 2001 as a way to reset the historical clock to Year Zero (Rashid 2001). You can't accomplish these follies without a lot of violence and murder — psychic, bodily, structurally, and otherwise. As one of my favorite novelists Lucy Corin has said, "When apocalyptic thinking is internal, it's rich and beautiful." But "enact [apocalyptic thinking] in real time with real people, and it's just about as fucked up as you can get" — because "of history, because there is no *new* time" (quoted in Vogrin 2010, 67; my emphasis). Nevertheless, an unthinking embrace of tradition for tradition's sake is equally dangerous, and novelty is important, if only to help us unsettle some of our overly-habituated modes of thought and practice. We'll admit, then, that we can't escape history and that Epicurus's laminar void, through which atomic particles once "rained," and then, through which various small "swerves" (Luctretius's *clinamen*) created our world, is no longer possible (at least, not from the standpoint of the universe being empty and unformed). At the same time, we need to somehow be able to cultivate a certain radical contingency in order to engender material encounters that can't be predicted in advance, and out of which alternative life and art practices become more possible. The very problem of politics, in my opinion, is precisely its entrenchment in mentalities and histories and procedures that can't be, or aren't allowed to be, unthought nor abandoned (on this point, see Althusser 2006). But we can't reboot democracy, either, by hitting the delete key and just "starting over."

I honestly worry less about the destructive entrenchment of bad "un-novel" and acquiescent politics and more about the ways in which transnational, hyper-runaway capital makes even political regimes ultimately inconsequential relative to "how things might turn out" (with respect to climate change, sectarian wars, the automation of human labor, the end of the public research university as we have known it, global poverty and the scarcity of vital resources such as clean water, environmental pollution and pandemics, etc.). And with Aranye, I neither want to avoid lack and discontinuity nor continuity and resurgence. Nor do I want to despair, although, as Robin Mackay and Armen Avanessian have written in their Introduction to the *#Accelerate#* reader,

> Despair seems to be the dominant sentiment of the contemporary Left, whose crisis perversely mimics its foe, consoling itself either with the minor pleasures of shrill denunciation, mediatised protest and ludic disruptions, or with the scarcely credible notion that maintaining a grim "critical" vigilance on the total subsumption of human life under capital, from the safehouse of theory, or from within contemporary art's self-congratulatory fog of "indeterminacy," constitutes resistance. (2014, 5)

I also do not believe, strictly speaking, that there is any longer (nor has there ever been) an Outside to depart to, some other ground on which entirely new structures could be built apart from toxic hyper-capitalist relations, although I think about betrayal a lot, and about the importance of irresponsibility, with regard to both tradition *and* innovation, and also with regard to plotting a certain course that supposedly knits both together into the form of a so-called ethical or "good" life. As Sara Ahmed has put it, "For a life to count as a good life […] it must return the debt of its life by taking on the direction promised as a social good, which means imagining one's futurity in terms of reaching certain points along a life course. A queer life might be one that fails to make such gestures of return" (2006, 21). We can't stop looking back, or forward, but we might refuse to take on certain inheritances, no matter from which direction they're arriving — the past, with its "traditions," and the future, with its supposedly inevitable neoliberal accelerationism and resulting technological singularities (see Williams and Srnicek 2013).

I'm interested, then, in gestures of refusal, of non-compliance, of (again) betrayal, and in thinking about the ways in which the present might be more of a creatively productive fugitive zone, where time forks and bends everywhere *but* the past and future, and where we might practice the arts of divergent, tapestried becomings. As Aranye writes in "(Dis)continuity: A History of Dreaming," "Somehow, the unpredictable depends on what it supersedes. We cannot bypass having a past," and yet, at the same time, "the work is to keep moving" (Fradenburg 2009, 93, 109).

So, yes, let us not necessarily undo, nor blow up, what we have learned thus far, but let us definitely diverge. Although, contra Aranye, I want to put in a good word for occasionally "bearing to *stay*" where we might happen to be at any given moment, even if it's the most fucked-up place imaginable — not as a refusal of movement or change or productively divergent becomings, but as a form of resistance to the idea that the only good movement is forward, or somewhere else other than here, wherever that may be. Maybe there are times when we should embrace being stuck in personal incapacities and what might be called inoperative communities[4] of the exhausted, of institutionalized (and even post-institutionalized) invalids, where we might allow ourselves to be "at an impasse," while also cultivating new arts of care and convalescence, rest and indolence, choosing *not to perform* versus learning how to perform at ever more high and supposedly calculable levels. I borrow these notions from Jan Verwoert, who also asks us to consider what it might mean to embrace an "existential exuberance," which would be

> a way to perform without any mandate or legitimation, in response to the desires and dreams of other people, but without the aim or pretense of merely fulfilling an existing demand. It is always a way of giving too much of what is not presently requested. It is a way of giving what you do not have to others who may not want it. It is a way of transcending your capacities by embracing your incapacities and therefore a way to interrupt the brute assertiveness of the *I Can* through the performance of an *I Can't* performed in the key of *I Can*. It's a way of insisting that, even if we can't get it now, we can get it, in some other way at some other point in time. (2007, 94)

4 I borrow the term "inoperative community" from Jean-Luc Nancy, who writes that community is "given to us [...] well in advance of all our projects, desires, and undertakings," and further, that, at bottom, community is resistance itself, especially resistance to immanence (1991, 35). The essence of a community we could really get behind (and that would not harden into fascism) is its own "incessant incompletion" and the way it ceaselessly "exposes community *at its limit*" (1991, 38; Nancy's emphasis).

That sounds like a good definition of teaching to me as well, although I myself have stopped teaching — have stopped being a "professor" — partly because the university, increasingly, feels less and less like an hospitable place in which to think, write, and share ideas. It doesn't feel like the right place any more to enact what Lauren Berlant has called the "becoming-impasse," or the "collaborative risk of a shared disorganization," where "it is possible to value floundering around with others whose attention-paying to what's happening is generous and makes liveness possible as a good, not a threat" (2011, 85–86). But I still care about the fate of the public university, and that goes back to not wanting to blow things up. I just don't know sometimes if the university is the place any more to work on the university.

Much of my own academic career (whatever that word "career" might mean) has been torn between: (a) wanting to reform the university from within (where the glacial pace of change and seemingly endemic cowardice and personally petty antipathies have mainly dispirited me), and (b) wanting to escape its techno-managerial-bureaucratic controls completely in order to found and enact something radically Other, something more faithful to Derrida's "university without condition," which Derrida believed would "remain an ultimate place of critical resistance — and more than critical — to all the powers of dogmatic and unjust appropriation," and which had special safekeeping by way of the humanities, entailing the "principal right to say everything, whether it be under the heading of fiction and the experimentation of knowledge, and the right to say it publicly, to publish it" (2001, 26). Of course this is a utopian view, but I believe the university, in a sense, has always been utopian and never really actualized. We may bemoan the hyperbolic corporatization of the University, where we hardly have time any more to simply read, think, write, and teach thanks to never-ending rounds of assessment protocols, and where the defunding of humanities programs continues apace with the adjunctification of teaching lines and an obscenely staggering level of national student loan debt, but the University has always been, in some sense, a bureaucratic institution — its very "institution-ality" and various modes and protocols of professionalization of disciplinary knowledge necessarily created (and sustains) a situation where, as Foucault once argued,

> the production of discourse is at once controlled, selected, organized and redistributed according to a certain number of procedures, whose role is to avert its powers and its dangers, to cope with chance events, to evade its ponderous, awesome materiality. [...] We all know perfectly well that we are not free to just say anything, that we cannot simply speak of anything, when we like or where we like; not just anyone, finally, may speak of just anything. (1972, 216)

So perhaps the University-to-come is one of those chance (and precarious) events with which we must now cope (and also cultivate). Could we perhaps embrace a deterritorialization of the University, some sort of exodus that is not an escape from obligation(s) because it is also intent on inventing a common world as "a space of horizontal negotiations without arbiter" (Bourriaud 2009, 188)? This might entail going "radicant" — Nicolas Bourriaud's term for "setting one's roots in motion, staging them in heterogeneous contexts and formats, denying them the power to completely define one's identity, translating ideas, transcoding images, transplanting behaviors, exchanging rather than imposing." One has roots (a past, certain inheritances, etc.), but they are always on the move, "effacing their origin(s) in favor of simultaneous or successive enrootings" (Bourriaud 2009, 22). This effacement could be painful, of course, even sad — yet nevertheless, roots remain, in place, while also being transitive. You can have your *place,* and move it, too. Same goes for the classroom, which could be anywhere, while still being rooted in what Bill Readings called the "university in ruins." In other words, there is still a University (with a capital "U") to which we are dedicated, but it isn't the transnational corporation most of us work in today; rather, it is a collective commitment to *spending time* in *"listening to Thought"* — one which resists commodification and which always keeps "meaning open as a locus of debate," and there will never be a "homogeneous standard of value that might unite all poles of the pedagogical scene so as to produce a single scale of evaluation" of *that* situation (Readings 1996, 165).

Of course, as Aranye rightly points out, there are important issues of attachment to work through when considering where we might want to place ourselves vis-à-vis learning and teaching, thinking and writing. But isn't there also a productive sort of mourning always attendant upon learning, where one has to lose, or let go of (and then re-find in other spectral and material forms) something practically every day? I used to always tell my students that they should want to know more, but they would also have to accept that knowing things entails being sad and embracing one's fucked-up-ness, precisely because of that complexity Aranye describes — yes, complex systems always build on pre-existing materials, but something new is always emerging, and the ground is always moving under your feet. You couldn't stand still, even if you wanted to. There are no certainties, no unchanging verities. Learning is already unlearning, a continual upending of everything you thought you knew, and therefore, difficult and melancholic, especially when it requires you to let go of something you thought you couldn't live without. And no one said we had to let go of everything. With Stephen White, I believe in the "sustaining" affirmations of weak ontologies — "strong beliefs, weakly held." Our "figurations of self, other, and beyond-human are never purely cognitive matters; rather they are always aesthetic–affective," yet a weak ontologist recognizes that "no one set of figurations can claim universal, self-evident truth" (White 2005, 17). Commitments matter, figurations matter, but we must carry these life-goods lightly.

I agree that we have to also consider that "tear in the fabric of the Real" (whether climate change catastrophe or even just the "ruin" of the university as "public trust") and whether or not, similar to that tribe for whom the Elders have been wiped out, there is "irreparable damage" to our "capacity for making and responsiveness," or there is still "opportunity to innovate." Another way to put this might be, "what do we hope for now" (as learners, as teachers)? As Jonathan Lear explicates beautifully in *Radical Hope: Ethics in the Face of Cultural Devastation,* "as finite erotic creatures it is an essential part of our nature that we take risks just by being the world," and the world itself is not "merely the environment in which we move about"; rather, "it is that over which we lack omnipotent control," and at any moment, it "may intrude upon us," outstripping "the concepts with which we seek to understand it" (2006, 120). So, in merely *thinking* the world, we always take the risk "that the very concepts with which we think may become unintelligible" (Lear 2006, 116). In such a scenario, learning might then be a form of radical hope — not hope as an affective (and ultimately insipid) orientation toward definitive (projected-in-advance) outcomes, but rather, hope as a longing, or desire, for things that we do not fully, and cannot ever fully, understand. There would thus always be a dialogic struggle as well (which could also be a form of friendship) — learning as the sort of encounter modeled by Lauren Berlant and Lee Edelman in *Sex, or the Unbearable,* where dialogue "commits us to grappling with negativity, non-sovereignty, and social relation not only as abstract concepts but also as the substance and condition of our responses — and our responsibilities — to each other" (Berlant and Edelman 2013, ix), and I would add, to the world more largely. And the university-to-come would constitute a collective project for which there is no foreseeable future, but on behalf of which future, we can agree — while we continue to disagree about all sorts of things — that at least we *care.*

Infinitely Enmeshed

What if we spread out our ideas and knowledge and signifiers and everything else on a Deleuzo-Guattarian surface, such that nothing is either old or new, past or present? What would we want from such plenty? What would we lose by giving up temporality, irreversibility, yearning, the *affective* categories of past, present, and future? I think maybe we would lose some of the richness and variety of our affective states and transformations.

For more than a century, analysts have been devoted to the "frame": the combination of the office, regular appointments, and financial regulations that ideally create a "holding environment" for the patient. I respect what this structure can accomplish for many patients, partly because it's a structure that evokes the death drive. Further, most analysts today know that the world is *in* the office and the office is *in* the world, and that transmission and transference transform without appreciable limit. These are material facts and effects. Eco-psychoanalysis and psychotherapy are now beginning to think more deliberately about how awareness of our infinite enmeshment with all forms of matter should change clinical practice, and as I'm sure you know, are beginning to advocate for and practice psychotherapy "outside" the office, in the forests, atop mountains, and by the beautiful sea. I welcome this probing of boundaries, these topological enactments. I do not myself anticipate ever practicing by hiking; my view is that if we care about the nature-that-is-no-longer-Nature, it's best we stay out of it. But the single most important thing for any creature to learn, through education or psychoanalysis, or caring or being cared for, is that it is a mortal creature, ever-changing, yet in its organic form subject to the limit of death, constitutively vulnerable to affecting and being affected because of its aliveness. The joys of creatureliness — the sensory and other sensitivities that are also the source of our vulnerability — are equally important in re-situating ourselves in a post-Guattarian world. I am not opposed to going "outside"; there are many ways to go "outside" the clinic and the university, too. I just don't want to go Outward Bound. The issue I want to address is how we now conceive phenomenologically of the topology of the relationships among classrooms, clinics, inner and outer worlds — especially because my interlocutor Eileen has been such a visionary creator of de-institutionalizing processes and practices.

The classroom is unquestionably an intersubjective, transpersonal space/event. What are its therapeutic possibilities, given that group therapy techniques are not appropriate in the nonetheless highly groupified scene of *academic* learning? One of my former professors once said to me that asking students how they *felt* about a poem or whatever was an *ipso facto* admission of pedagogical incompetence. Given what we have learned about perceptions and affects in the intervening years, I am now sure he was wrong. In the humanities and fine arts, we can help our students *think* about what feelings are, how feelings work, what kinds of intelligence they represent, and why they are often so difficult either to communicate to, or hide from, other beings. At the same time, we help them "see," "hear," and "touch" — what do images evoke in us, what is the intonational *range* of a line of verse, and why, and where does a poem place us? Our topics and teaching methods can emphasize the integration of thinking and symbolizing with affect and sensation, and in this way, help us all learn about the learning process as we go. All facts and ideas have valence, both "positive" and "negative," as the psychologists so lyrically put it. Learning ought to include awareness of this principle. If Texan students need to "unlearn" the idealized version of US history they are now taught in high school when they get to college or university, I believe this process must include mourning, helping them to understand that knowledge and knowledge production have valence, that we all become *attached* to particular narratives, conceptualizations, and beliefs, and that we understand them better when we understand how and why we are attached to them. So we can ask students about the range of feelings inspired in them by specific concepts (and vice-versa), lived experience, and literary texts. We can help our students cultivate and enjoy the crucial *real-time activities* of interpretation and expression that make relationships — economic, political, personal — possible in the first place. We can help them value error, failure, and surprise. And we can help them work through the ideas and attitudes that severely limit the potentiality and richness of their life experience.

We can introduce our students to the mind's real-time efforts to know itself, the world, and the minds of others — to see that the mind's waywardness is part and parcel of its plasticity, that our species has learned to talk about feelings as a way of making enabling use of them, that the ambiguities of language are precisely what give it its powers of connectivity, in the form of the "spreading activations" Norman Holland (2009) discusses in *Literature and the Brain,* earlier called by Freud "associational pathways." We can say things like *"think,"* while pulling on our hair, to illustrate embodiment. We can show them how free association can begin a new thinking process, and how imagining, loving, and hating are aspects of remembering. There's nothing like the real time of live classroom experience for learning more about the everyday mental and emotional activities on which surviving and thriving depend. The best way to teach students about their minds is to ask them to use them in situations that demand improvisation and colloquy — that is to say, in everyday life — regardless of whether one is lecturing or teaching a small seminar. Affects belong in the classroom — again, I am speaking of the importance of integrating affect and cognition — as does the time required to reflect on them. Interpreting the minds of others is a precious survival skill many millions of years in the making, and its practice is (therefore) a source of joy. Intersubjectivity is necessary to, if not sufficient for, learning, and that is what makes live classtime experience so precious and difficult to simulate. The classroom is an ecology, but like all ecologies, infinitely enmeshed in many many others.

The Affinity of Thought

How we might conceive of the topology of the relationship between the classroom and the clinic, especially with the possible joys to be derived from encountering other minds (and I would add, other forms of sentience — human *and* nonhuman, whether embodied in real time, in the realm of the aesthetic, etc.), feels important to me, too. Both the classroom and the clinic are (or could be) critical sites for cultivating the arts and *technē* of the care of the self, for working on ourselves to "invent," and not to "discover," as Foucault once remarked, "improbable manners of being" and new "affective intensities" that might "yield […] relations not resembling those that are institutionalized" (1996, 310). This has something to do as well with philosophy — increasingly, one of our most marginalized disciplines within the humanities — yet could anything be more essential to learning, and to the university, since philosophy, or critical theory, names the practice of what Bill Readings called "thought beside itself" (1996, 192), or what Leo Bersani has described as a lifelong devotion to "intrinsically unending" discussions, or, "to put it not quite so dryly, to spiritually liquefying speech" (2008a, 87)? This is "a special kind of talk unconstrained by consequences other than further talk," a type of "conversation suspended in virtuality" that, similar to the psychoanalytic relation, treats the unconscious "not as the determinant depth of being but, instead, as de-realized being, as never more than potential being" (Bersani 2008b, 28). This "talk" also entails what Aranye has called elsewhere a "shared attention" that is a "consequence of attachment" and of "intersubjective play," and which is always about "becoming" and never about "finishing" (Fradenburg 2011, 62, 57). Both the classroom and the clinic, as well as the signifying arts, as Aranye has described them in various writings, invite an "affective companionship" in which "we never finish working things out," but that doesn't mean we don't accomplish anything (Fradenburg 2011, 50). Such sites also require what Aranye has called "friendly" yet impersonal minds: "extimate" figures who enact a sort of "disinterested pastoral care" (healers, narrators, therapists, teachers), and who, in premodern narratives, were "always liminally situated — in homes not their own, woods and clearings, anonymous *thropes,* away from the main business of the day" (Fradenburg 2011, 59).

Away from the main business of the day — what, today, might it mean to live and practice pedagogic relations as forms of care of the self and affective (non-possessive) companionship in the liminal spaces so necessary for engendering productive encounters with other "friendly" minds, and with error, failure, and surprise? The university, I believe, has become increasingly hostile toward such liminal spaces, such encounters, and such non-calculable events, and it is increasingly insisting that everything, in fact, be "worked out," and in a business-like fashion that feels very antithetical to the idea that knowledge should remain perpetually unsettled (that "learning," in fact, is always "unlearning"). I believe that the university, and its classrooms, will continue to be important sites for keeping open the question of thought and for fostering various important modes of affectively-wired cognitive experiments, but I also think it is time for a subterfugitive, vagabond, rogue para-academy, especially when so many of us are hanging on to the university by the skin of our teeth (and minds). We might even distinguish between the University (as a certain institution of knowledge communication) and Academia (as knowledge communication itself), between which there is no necessary connection. As Paul Boshears has put it, "Both the University and Academia are imagined communities, to borrow Benedict Anderson's phrase. However, the University is an institution that accredits, controls, and stamps the passport of those who would enter its territory. It is a striated space as opposed to Academia's [more] fluid space" (quoted in Allen et al. 2012, 139). I don't know if I myself completely buy into this distinction (I've always been of the camp that everything is so intermeshed that trying to draw lines is just futile), but I would like to see scholars absconding with the University (with, in other words, its academic "contraband"), in order to practice a polyglot, cosmopolitan pedagogy that would enunciate a "shaggy heart" and have "no fixed abode" (Kristeva 1994, 140).

"Frames" matter, of course, and as Aranye points out, the classroom (as well as the therapist's office) serve as important "holding environments," but if the mind's "waywardness is part and parcel of its plasticity," then can we not also engage a wandering pedagogy — not necessarily in the style of Outward Bound (I don't like hauling canoes, or hiking, myself, either), but in terms of having the courage to either depart the existing institution in order to form new desiring-assemblages and new environments for our embodied pedagogies (however we might envision them) or to hunker down within the institution itself while also refusing to comply with the baroquely deadening "effectiveness" protocols and "cost-to-benefits" analyses dreamed up by the ever-increasing ranks of the university's managerial technocrats? Perhaps teaching within the institution has always been, in some sense, adversarial and subversive with respect to the university's administrators, if even quietly so (because under the radar, behind a closed door, largely undocumented, and in many respects, unremarked upon). And there is something importantly private and intimate (while also impersonal) about the pedagogic scene, no matter how publicly situated. I am reminded of something Lyotard wrote in 1978 about his experience teaching philosophy at Vincennes in a beautiful, yet somewhat despairing essay, "Endurance and the Profession." At the time that Lyotard wrote this essay, the philosophy faculty had lost the right to grant degrees, and yet students were still showing up to study philosophy there. Christopher Fynsk has referred to Lyotard's anguished reflections on his teaching at that time as a "pedagogy on the verge of disaster" (2013). Here is Lyotard:

> The concessions to what you feel is expected become rarer. You'd like to neglect even what your own mind desires, make it accessible to thoughts it doesn't expect. […] You are unfaithful in your alliances like the barbarians of Clastres, but for a different reason, opposite at least. You're at war with institutions of your own mind and your own identity. And you know that with all this, you're probably only perpetuating Western philosophy, its laborious libertinage, and its obliging equanimity. At least you also know that the only chance (or mischance) to do so lies in setting philosophy beside itself. (1993, 75–76)

When I myself read these words, I experienced something of a shock as I recognized in the words "setting philosophy beside itself" an echo with Bill Readings's description of the University-to-come as the place where we simply place Thought beside itself — thoughts alongside other thoughts — without ever asserting the need for consensus (or even for departments that would ultimately sediment, and strangulate, Thought over time). Then I also noticed that Readings was the editor of Lyotard's collected political writings, in which "Endurance and the Profession" is included, and thus the "impress" of Lyotard's writing upon Readings's own writing also impressed itself upon my own consciousness with a certain tender vibration.

And I trace this line of affinity of thought to also say, or claim, that the University-to-come must also be a place of the affinity of Thought, where Thought continually suspends itself in its encounters with Other Thought, by it which it is always limned and bordered. This affinity would, of necessity, be a difficult affinity, but it would still be affinity, a closeness and intimacy that is important, because chosen freely, between ourselves, whether inside of the classroom or outside of it. This would be a pedagogy of rogue desires (or thoughts) meeting, in the forest, with other rogue desires (or thoughts). Everything would be in suspension, and in contact, simultaneously. Unworking thought, while also "working it," would be our aim. It would always be dusk. The conversation would never end.

Going Outdoors

Yes, topological intricacy matters in the thinking of un/learning. Going "outdoors" to an outdoors that isn't necessarily concrete, but can be. Going "outdoors" not to learn that we can survive in Nature unassisted, but so that we can cultivate sentience, i.e., sense, feel, and enjoy our creatureliness. In the virtual extimacy of the mindscape, anything can happen, just as the extimacy of the outdoors is a realm of *possibility*. What is in me is also in whatever surrounds me, and *vice-versa*. Learning is what we *do*; therapeutic opportunities are everywhere. How might we best design, enrich, enable changes of embodied, environed minds? We have here, for example, a platform for newly creative thinking about how we might deliver "alternative" skills to graduate students who can't or don't choose to become professors, so that we might open the university to the kinds of learning and "working through" enabled by movement and making, enacting as well as acting. "Skills" or "arts and crafts" only sound boring because we have scorned for so long the materiality associated with them, preferring the more putatively spiritual pursuits of theory. But action and movement, according to the philosophers and neuroscientists, is looking less and less cognitively-deprived and more and more like the very ground of cognition itself. If we can use theory to cultivate and maintain awareness of what is entailed in action and enactment, we will be able to frame psychoanalysis quite differently, and perhaps open up for ourselves the enjoyments entailed in *all* the kinds of work we do.

REFERENCES

Ahmed, S. (2006). *Queer Phenomenology: Orientations, Objects, Others*. Durham: Duke University Press.

Allen, J. et al. (2012). "Discussions Before an Encounter." *continent*. 2.2: 136–47.

Althusser, L. (2006). "The Underground Current of the Materialism of the Encounter." In *Philosophy of the Encounter: Later Writings, 1978–87*, eds. F. Matheron and O. Corpet, trans. G.M. Goshgarian 163–207. London: Verso.

Andreasen, N. (2006). *The Creative Brain: The Science of Genius*. New York: Plume.

Bennett, J. (2001). *The Enchantment of Modern Life: Attachments, Crossing and Ethics*. Princeton: Princeton University Press.

Berlant, L. (2011). "Starved." In *After Sex? Writing Since Queer Theory*, eds. J. Halley and A. Parker, 79–90. Durham: Duke University Press.

——— and L. Edelman. (2014). *Sex, or the Unbearable*. Durham: Duke University Press.

Bersani, L. (2008a). "The Power of Evil and the Power of Love." In L. Bersani and A. Phillips, *Intimacies*, 57–87. Chicago: University of Chicago Press.

———. (2008b). "The It in the I." In L. Bersani and A. Phillips, *Intimacies*, 1–30. Chicago: University of Chicago Press.

Bion, W.R. (1959). "Attacks on Linking." *International Journal of Psycho-Analysis* 40: 308–15.

———. (1962). "A Theory of Thinking." *International Journal of Psycho-Analysis* 43: 306–10.

Bourriaud, N. (2009). *The Radicant.* New York: Lukas & Sternberg.

City Attorney of San Francisco. (2016). "City College." http://www.sfcityattorney.org/category/news/city-college/.

Damasio, A. (2010). *Self Comes to Mind: Constructing the Conscious Brain.* New York: Pantheon.

Deleuze, G. and F. Guattari. (1987). *A Thousand Plateaus: Capitalism and Schizophrenia,* trans. B. Massumi. Minneapolis: University of Minnesota Press.

Derrida, J. (2001). "The Future of the Profession or the University without Condition (thanks to the 'Humanities,' what could take place tomorrow)." In *Jacques Derrida and the Humanities: A Critical Reader,* ed. T. Cohen, 24–57. Cambridge: Cambridge University Press.

Descartes, R. ([1641] 1955). *Meditations on First Philosophy.* In *The Philosophical Works of Descartes,* Vol. 1, eds. and trans. E. Haldane and G. Ross. New York: Dover Publications.

Dias, B.G. and K.J. Ressler (2013). "Parental Olfactory Experience Influences Behavior and Neural Structure in Subsequent Generations." *Nature Neuroscience* 17: 89–96; doi:10.1038/nn.3594.

Edelman, G.M. (2004). *Wider than the Sky: The Phenomenal Gift of Consciousness.* New Haven: Yale University Press.

Foucault, M. (1972). *The Archaeology of Knowledge and The Discourse on Language,* trans. A.M.S. Smith. New York: Pantheon Books.

———. (1996). "Friendship As a Way of Life." In *Foucault Live (Interviews, 1961–1984),* ed. S. Lotringer, 308–12. New York: Semiotext(e).

Fradenburg, A. (2009). "(Dis)continuity: A History of Dreaming." In *The Post-Historical Middle Ages,* eds. E. Scala and S. Frederico, pp. 87–115. New York: Palgrave Macmillan.

Fradenburg, L.O.A. (2011). "Living Chaucer." *Studies in the Age of Chaucer* 33: 41–64.

———. (2013). *Staying Alive: A Survival Manual for the Liberal Arts,* ed. E.A. Joy. Brooklyn: punctum books.

Freud, S. (1961). "Letter from Sigmund Freud to Ludwig Binswanger, April 11, 1929." In *Letters of Sigmund Freud, 1873-1939,* ed. E.L. Freud, trans. T. Stern and J. Stern, 386. London: Hogarth Press.

———. (1955). "Beyond the Pleasure Principle." In *The Standard Edition of the Complete Psychological Works of Sigmund Freud,* Vol. 18: *Beyond the Pleasure Principle, Group Psychology and Other Works (1920-1922),* ed. and trans. J. Strachey, 1-64. London: Hogarth Press.

Fynsk, Christopher (2013). "A Pedagogy on the Verge of Disaster." In *Pedagogies of Disaster,* ed. Vincent W.J. van Gerven Oei, Adam Staley Groves, and Nico Jenkins, 37-48. Brooklyn, punctum books.

Holland, N. (2009). *Literature and the Brain.* Gainesville: The PsyArt Foundation.

Jones, P.H. (2010). *Introducing Neuroeducational Research: Neuroscience, Education and the Brain from Contexts to Practice.* New York: Routledge.

Jordan, M. (2012). "Did Lacan Go Camping? Psychotherapy in Search of an Ecological Self." In *Vital Signs: Psychological Responses to the Ecological Crisis,* eds. M.J. Rust and N. Totton, 33-45. London: Karnac.

Kristeva, J. (1994). *Strangers to Ourselves,* trans. L. Roudiez. New York: Columbia University Press.

Kuhn, T. (1962). *The Structure of Scientific Revolutions.* Chicago: University of Chicago Press.

Lear, J. (2006). *Radical Hope: Ethics in the Face of Cultural Devastation.* Cambridge, MA: Harvard University Press.

Lyotard, J.-F. (1993). "Endurance and the Profession." In *Political Writings,* trans. B. Readings and K.P. Geiman, 70-76. Minneapolis: University of Minnesota Press.

Mackay, R. and A. Avanessian. (2014). "Introduction." In *#Accelerate#,* eds. R. Mackay and A. Avanessian, 1-46. Falmouth: Urbanomic, 2014.

Margulis, L. (1998). *Symbiotic Planet: A New Look at Evolution.* New York: Basic Books.

Maturana, H.R. and F.J. Varela. ([1972] 1980). *Autopoeisis and Cognition: The Realization of the Living.* Dordrecht, Holland: Reidel Publishing.

Nancy, J.-L. (1991). *The Inoperative Community,* ed. P. Connor, trans. P. Connor, L. Garbus, M. Holland, and S. Sawhney. Minneapolis: University of Minnesota Press.

Petroski, H. (1992). *To Engineer is Human: The Role of Failure in Successful Design.* New York: Vintage.

Rashid, A. (2001, 12 March). "After 1,700 Years, Buddhas Fall to Taliban Dynamite." *The Telegraph.* http://www.telegraph.co.uk/news/worldnews/asia/afghanistan/1326063/After-1700-years-Buddhas-fall-to-Taliban-dynamite.html.

Readings, B. (1996). *The University in Ruins.* Cambridge, MA: Harvard University Press.

Singer, W. (2008). "Epigenesis and Brain Plasticity in Education." In *The Educated Brain: Essays in Neuroeducation,* eds. A.M. Battro, K.W. Fischer, and P.J. Lena, 97–109. Cambridge: Cambridge University Press.

Sodré, I. (1994). "Obsessional Certainty Versus Obsessional Doubt: From Two to Three." *Psychoanalytic Inquiry* 14: 379–92.

Srnicek, N. and A. Williams. (2013, May). "#ACCELERATE: Manifesto for an Accelerationist Politics." http://accelerationism.files.wordpress.com/2013/05/williams-and-srnicek.pdf.

Starbuck, W. (1996). "Unlearning Ineffective or Obsolete Technologies." *International Journal of Technologies.* http://archive.nyu.edu/fda/bitstream/2451/14188/1/IS-97-30.pdf.

Tokuhama-Espinosa, T. (2011). *Mind, Brain, and Education Science: A Comprehensive Guide to the New Brain-Based Teaching.* New York: W.W. Norton.

Verwoert, J. (2008). "Exhaustion and Exuberance: Ways to Defy the Pressure to Perform." In *Art Sheffield 08: Yes, No and Other Options* [exhibition pamphlet], 90–112. Sheffield: Sheffield Contemporary Art Forum.

Vogrin, V. (2010). "Ten Questions for Lucy Corin" [interview]. *Sou'wester* 38.2: 67–70.

White, S.D. (2005). "Weak Ontology: Geneaology and Related Issues." *The Hedgehog Review* 7.2: 11–25.

7

After-word(s)

Aidan Seery

The gentle but firm respect due to words eloquently spoken requires, I think, that we consider other forms of human activity in response to the essays in this book, rather than adding too many more words. Afterwords can often take the form of weighing-up, critiquing, evaluating, comparing and contrasting what has gone before, but here this is left to others to do so, as they hopefully will, in reviews, in further citing analyses, and in conversation.

No, my intention is not to provide an academic summary but a short editorial indulgence that reflects on the "after" of the essays presented here and the Dublin conference that gave rise to them. I will structure it using the slight conceit of the structure of "afterword." First, in the "aft" of this undertaking, in the sense of the "at the back and in the rear" of this book, lies an extraordinary extent of human engagement in the forms of intellectual and academic engagement, of physical and organizational activity, and of the establishment and nourishing of relationships. In a culture of avoidance of dualisms of mind and body, physical and mental, and the dubious valorizations attached to them, it is important to regard each of these forms of engagement as valuable, therefore a little word on each.

Much can be and hopefully will be said about the intellectual and academic engagement that this conference and book seeded and provoked. For one, it has sparked in many of us a new hope for educational theory and its place in an often reductive, stifling discourse about education and its purposes. There would seem to be at least one path towards a "re-*Bildung*" in educational theory and it is signposted and marked out in these essays.

The physical and organizational activity necessary to bring an exceptional group of people together for this book and the conference is also an educational act of considerable value. There should be, and I believe there was in the case of this project, a special felt quality about a gathering of educators and educationalists that is perhaps not shared by other groups of academics. As a result of a common interest in the way in which human beings negotiate meaning and action in the world and negotiate meaning and the actions of their own selves, educators tend to view each other also in a way that arouses a professional as well as a personal curiosity and interest in the other. The physical presence of one another at a conference, the act of listening to the spoken voice, the experience of feelings of elation, dejection, tiredness, joy, and hurt in the presence of others has a different quality to that provoked by reading the written word. On the other hand, many of the physical reactions felt were as a result of deep engagement in thought and questioning on the written material to be found in this book, and there is a sense in which the "learning" or "unlearning" of the conference/book can be seen in the way in which, in a Žižekian sense, the one is not an addition or a "beyond" to the other but a subtraction; the subtraction of the phantom that the one is prior to the other in anything but a chronological way, nor is one a fulfilment of the other. It is much more the case, the conference and book must be seen as dynamically "self-mediating" in themselves.

Finally, to the "aft" of this book there lies a matrix of relationships that initiated, supported, and completed the project as a whole and which can also be seen as an educational (as learning and unlearning) engagement in its own right. Learning/unlearning is rarely a solitary pursuit or event, and it is fitting that this book is a collaborative effort of thought-exchange, debate, confirmation, and re-assessment as authors prepared, presented, discussed, and then wrote finally for this publication. In particular the role of negation-in-relationship that occurs when people "co-front" and confront their ideas together seems to me to be central to the idea of learning/unlearning and to this undertaking as a whole.

Perhaps it may be claimed that a consideration of what lies both to the "aft" of this book together with what now appears to the reader between these covers lend themselves to the conclusion that what is recorded here has the nature of an "educational event" of learning/unlearning, as also sketched in Éamonn's introduction to "unlearning" in this volume. Without venturing into any further discussion of the understanding, place, or importance of a currently favoured concept in philosophy for the field of education, the occurrence of this book and the conference that brought these authors to one place can be seen as a rupture in the inertia of what is deemed the "commonsensical" status quo of thinking in education, dominated by the "big Other" of late capitalist ideology of education as workplace preparation and readiness. Perhaps it can be hoped that this conference/book represents an event (Badiou) or an act (Žižek) that irrupts from within a stagnant status quo and that "sets in motion trajectories of transformation" (Johnston 2009, xxix).

Those involved in the hours of careful preparation of a conference or of meticulous and time-consuming editing of a text might well challenge this idea that what is happening here is an unexpected, explosive event. However, a glance to the phenomenological traits in Romano's hermeneutics of events suggest that our conference/book project on "unlearning" can indeed be interpreted as an educational event in its own right. For one, and by admission of those involved, the project has gripped, seduced, and drawn people in a deep way, calling on them to come into play in their complete selves. For some too, a new world of understanding and interpretation has been opened or established in a surprising and unexpected way out of the natural and ordinary lives of teaching and thinking that might have continued in well-trodden paths were it not for the intervention of this event. Then there is the evental experience that even though the idea of unlearning and the conference/book project might have appeared as a disruption in our thought and practice, they also give normative sense to the adventure of our teaching/learning lives. There is a peculiar and exciting and enlivening order in the disorder! Then, of course, there is the question of time and temporality in events. Clearly, the conference took place on dates and days and this book appears on a single day, but the event of being grasped by the "unlearning" idea in its embodiment and enactment in this project is something that indeed, in a way, stands outside of time, heralds and opens a new time. In all of these ways, our project might assume the position of an "event."

Finally, the afterwards of the afterwords should surely be given some small thought. Three "afters" at least suggest themselves for this book. The first is a renewed sense of *wonder* at the process and events of education as self-formation and transformation. The event reported here will hopefully surprise readers and even astonish some to the extent of acting in a new and creative way. As Spinoza has claimed in a thought that has been taken up also by Deleuze, there is a particular attraction to us of the singular, of how something like education and learning that we previously knew to be linked to other things in a commonsense way all of a sudden appears different, differently connected, and generates a desire to examine it again and see it in a totally new way.

A second "after" could be conceptualized using the idea from Malabou, that of the *disruption of identity* by singular and unexpected accidents. Perhaps this book can be seen as an accident, something that had no necessity in the order of things, but that has not only the power to create desire but is much more capable of actually disrupting at least professional identity. Learning/unlearning as presented here is not a pedagogical approach or technique that stands alongside others and that can be employed intentionally in the same way in the pursuit of pre-determined outcomes and purposes. The idea of learning/unlearning is at an ontological level that supersedes the power and autonomy of the teacher–subject in a startling and disturbing way and from the "outside."

The final ingredient to the "afters" of this conference/book is the invitation to action-thought. It is quite normal to claim that action must follow words, and indeed we hope that the wonder that follows the surprise of some of the things said here will indeed issue in action; in different ways of teaching and learning; in different ways of engaging with knowledge and students and of undertaking educational research. However, echoing again Éamonn's earlier words, I am acutely aware of the exhortation of Heidegger to *"think"* and of the warning from Žižek that what is called for in our present time is not action but thought. Especially in the field of education, there is a tendency to move too quickly to action, to prioritize the practical almost to the exclusion of theoretical considerations when, in fact, what is called for is thinking. Clearly, the kind of thinking envisaged is not of an instrumental nature even though we are dealing with matters of teaching and learning, but it is a thinking that "desires to be thought about" (Heidegger 1976, 6) and as a result provokes and elicits learning/unlearning. It is a thinking "that turns away from man. It withdraws from him" (Heidegger 1976, 8) but which we can hardly help follow, drawn as we are to the possibility that we might find authenticity in epiphany.

So let us be drawn to thinking, the learning/unlearning of thinking, and indeed the thinking of learning and unlearning.

In summary, it might not be too much to claim that the particular historical moment of the publication of this book has the potential to transform the story of educational theory and the life stories of a number of educators in a way that is not limited to an effect only in the present but changes both past and future. I, for one, see my past teaching and learning in a new way and certainly will teach, read, and learn in a different way in the future as a result of the engagement with learning/unlearning, the "Unlearning" conference, and the reading of these texts. I suspect and hope that I am not the only one changed in this way.

To return to the beginning, these are responses that go beyond words.

REFERENCES

Deleuze, G. (1994). *Difference and Repetition,* trans P. Patton. London: The Athlone Press.
Heidegger, M. (1979). *What is Called Thinking?* London: Harper Collins.
Johnston, A. (2009). *Badiou, Žižek, and Political Transformations: The Cadence of Change.* Evanston, IL: Northwestern University Press.
Malabou, C. (2012). *Ontology of the Accident: An Essay on Destructive Plasticity.* Cambridge: Polity.
Romano, C. (2009). *Event and World.* New York, NY: Fordham University Press.
Spinoza, B. (1997). *Ethics,* trans. A. Boyle. London: Dent.
Žižek, S. (2014). *The Most Sublime Hysteric: Hegel with Lacan.* Cambridge: Polity.

www.ingramcontent.com/pod-product-compliance
Lightning Source LLC
Chambersburg PA
CBHW072044160426
43197CB00014B/2623